MW00529590

Here the glorious gospel of (
here the gospel preacher is
and fully to all; and here the sinner is compelled to receive it
without objection or delay. Thoroughly biblical, confessionally
reformed, and winsomely written—a little gem of a book! Here
is warm-hearted Calvinism on full display!

Jonny Gibson
Associate Professor of Old Testament, Westminster Theological
Seminary, Philadelphia

Using his scholarly expertise on this subject, Donald John
MacLean has offered us a clear, accessible treatment of the
biblical teaching on the free offer of the gospel. Marshalling
Reformed luminaries from the past, with a sensitive pastoral
touch, Dr. MacLean has written a book that Pastors can enjoy
and also recommend to their flock. It is probably the best work
I have read of its kind.

Mark Jones
Senior Pastor at Faith Presbyterian Church (PCA), Vancouver,
Canada

John Calvin once preached that 'When we know God to be our
Father, should we not desire that he be known as such by all?
And if we do not have this passion, that all creatures do him
homage, is it not a sign that his glory means little to us?' This is
a relentlessly biblical and relentlessly open-hearted book, which
shows us very clearly that those who delight most in the truth of
God's glorious sovereignty should be passionate and persistent
evangelists—like Jesus.

Lee Gatiss
Director of Church Society and author of *Light After Darkness:
How the Reformers Regained, Retold, and Relied on the Gospel of Grace*

This superb new book deals with some very live questions amongst Reformed Christians: does God love everyone? Can we offer everyone the invitation to come to Christ? Can we urge, persuade and plead with everyone, as 'appointed agents' of the Lord Jesus? With careful and systematic use of Scripture, the author conclusively shows us that the answer is a resounding 'Yes'. I pray that this book spurs us all to make the free offer of the good news of Jesus Christ to everyone, with urgency, winsomeness, and power.

Jeremy Marshall
Evangelist and author of *Beyond the Big C: Hope in the Face of Death*

Words are important. Never more so than in a generation brought up without a knowledge of moral absolutes. Few words are more important, and when understood, less subjective, than 'gospel'. To understand it, to respond to it, and to communicate it accurately we must know what it means. Donald John MacLean helpfully lays out the biblical teaching on this most important of topics, and its implications. The chapter 'Objections considered' to the free offer of the gospel is particularly noteworthy. It is a welcome addition to writings in this field.

Alasdair Macleod
Minister, Smithton Free Church, Inverness, Scotland

The gospel of Jesus Christ is the greatest news the world has ever known. As Christians, we need to tell everyone about it. In this well-written book, Donald John MacLean expertly and concisely takes readers through the biblical, theological, and practical reasons why the gospel invitation is for all people. Along the way, he shows how belief in God's sovereignty informs our commitment to the free offer of the gospel. His tips for further reading will also reward anyone who takes the time to follow his recommendations. In the end, MacLean rightly calls us to study, know, and proclaim the glorious news that the message of salvation is for all people who repent of their sin and trust in Christ alone as He is freely offered to them in the gospel.

John W. Tweedale
Academic Dean and Professor of Theology,
Reformation Bible College, Sanford, Florida

In a day of cool communication, Donald John MacLean makes the case for warm, wholehearted and unrestrained gospel proclamation. Drawing deeply from the Scriptures, he shows that God, in His love for sinners, invites, pleads, sells, knocks, commands, warns, and promises through the preaching of the Gospel. This book made me want to preach. It is a treasure for all who love the gospel of Jesus Christ.

Colin S. Smith
Senior Pastor, The Orchard, Arlington Heights, Illinois
President, Unlocking the Bible

ALL THINGS ARE **READY**

Understanding the Gospel
in its Fullness and Freeness

DONALD JOHN MACLEAN

CONTENTS

To my Father.

'Is iad clann an cloinne coron sheann daoine; agus is iad an
athraichean urram cloinne.'
Gnàth-fhacail 17:6

***

It is on the crest of the wave of the divine sovereignty that the full
and free overtures of God's grace in Christ break upon the shores of
lost humanity.
John Murray (1898-1975)
Collected Writings of John Murray
(4 vols.; Edinburgh: Banner of Truth, 1976-1982), 1:146-7.

INTRODUCTION

God desires nothing more earnestly than that those who were perishing and rushing to destruction should return into the way of safety ... And for this reason ... the Gospel [is] spread abroad in the world.
John Calvin (1509-1564)[1]

It is one of the glories of the gospel that it is universal in scope. There is nothing narrow or limited about the good news of salvation. It is for 'all the nations' (Matt 28:19, c.f. Ps. 2:8, Ps. 96:1-3). This truth has inspired the great missionary movements of the Church, it has led to the world being turned upside down on many occasions (Acts 17:6), and it is still changing lives throughout the world today. Because of the universality of the gospel the day is coming when a 'great multitude which no one could number, of all nations, tribes, peoples, and tongues' will stand 'before the throne and before the Lamb, clothed with white robes' (Rev. 7:9).

My hope in this book is to explore this great gospel message of salvation, focusing on the nature of this free offer of the good news of salvation to lost sinners. By this free offer I mean a well

---

1. John Calvin, *Calvin's Commentaries* (22 vols.; Grand Rapids: Baker, 1981), 12:246.

meant and sincere invitation from God to all without exception to embrace Jesus Christ as Saviour. This gospel invitation is expressive of God's pleasure in the salvation of all to whom the gospel comes, and expresses grace and love to all who hear it whether they are saved or not. As John Murray has said, 'the gospel is not simply an offer or invitation but also implies that God delights that those to whom the offer comes would enjoy what is offered in all its fullness.'[2]

That we are committed to a gospel offer of this kind for all is important for many theological and pastoral reasons. On a cultural level we, in the western world, are living in a humanistic, secularised environment. The culture is against us in a way it has not been for centuries. The Church appears embattled. There is a danger of retreating in on ourselves, of simply being on a defensive footing concerned about maintaining the status quo. In contrast, the free offer of the gospel, and God's heart in the gospel offer, lifts up our heads and reminds us of the life-giving message we have for our weary, broken world. It calls us not to lose heart but, believing that the gospel remains 'the power of God to salvation' (Rom. 1:16), to take the message that 'commands all men everywhere to repent' (Acts 17:30) out into our communities and culture.

Theologically the gospel offer is important because it beautifully balances and complements a commitment to God's sovereignty. It is the uniform testimony of scripture that 'salvation is of the Lord' (Jonah 2:9) and that it is God who ultimately says, 'I will have mercy on whomever I will have mercy, and I will have compassion on whomever I will have compassion' (Rom. 9:15). There is no doubt of God's sovereign choice in salvation: 'I give them eternal life, and they shall never perish; neither shall anyone snatch them out of My hand'

---

2. John Murray, *Collected Writings of John Murray* (4 vols.; Edinburgh: Banner of Truth, 1976-1982), 4:114.

(John 10:28). However, an unbalanced commitment to God's sovereignty can lead us to hold distorted views of God as harsh and unloving, one who has no compassion for lost humanity. It can also lead us to become lethargic in our evangelism, for if God is sovereign, He will save His people anyway. But God's sovereignty and the gospel offer are companions not enemies. As Charles Spurgeon said, 'I once was asked to reconcile these two ... and I answered, "No, I never reconcile friends." These two ... never fell out: they are perfectly agreed.'[3] Holding to both God's sovereignty and gospel offer enables us to rejoice in God's sovereign kindness to all, and fires a desire to take the good news out to all, trusting that God's sovereignty will ensure 'such as should be saved' will be added to the Church (Acts 2:47, KJV).

Pastorally, a sincere gospel offer is crucial. Many individuals doubt God's concern for them. Perhaps they think they have sinned beyond hope of forgiveness. Or perhaps they think they need to make themselves more holy before they can come to God. Some who have grown up in churches committed to God's sovereignty might worry if they have a right to believe in Jesus, because God might not have chosen them to be saved. Over all these worries and concerns the gospel offer says, come to Jesus as you are. Put your concerns away. God wants you to embrace salvation. 'Believe on the Lord Jesus Christ, and you will be saved' (Acts 16:31).

In opening up the gospel offer in this book I will begin simply with defining the gospel. We need to be clear on what the good news we are offering to the world is. Then I will focus on God's sovereignty. That God is sovereign is our only hope that the gospel will be embraced. Having done that I expand on the definition of the gospel offer in this introduction, showing that

---

3. Charles Haddon Spurgeon, *The Metropolitan Tabernacle Pulpit Volume 30* (London: Passmore & Alabaster, 1885), 49.

the gospel offer is an invitation, a pleading, a command and much more. I then spend time showing that God truly offers the gospel to all without exception and encourages all to accept it. Then, turning to more theologically intricate matters, I will explore why it is right to say that God desires all to accept the gospel offer, and that the gospel offer expresses God's common grace and love. The book concludes by giving attention to some of the common objections (theological and pastoral) to the free offer of the gospel.

All these topics are covered with the overarching hope that Christians will be encouraged in the days we live in to share the good news. May churches and Christians who rejoice in the sovereignty of God never allow that to hedge in the gospel, and its call to all people: 'Come, for all things are now ready' (Luke 14:17).

1

WHAT IS THE GOSPEL?

It is Christ in all the glory of his person and in all the perfection of his finished work whom God offers in the gospel.
John Murray (1898-1975)[1]

What is the gospel? This might on one level seem the simplest of questions. It is 'glad tidings' (*euangelion*). It is the good news of salvation. But this is also the most profound and glorious of questions. To outline the gospel is to touch on many of the most important issues we can ever face: sin, salvation, the holiness of God and the mercy of God. Clarity on this point is essential because increasingly terms such as gospel, good news and evangelical have been emptied of meaning. Self-professed evangelicals disagree over what the condition of humanity before God as sinners is, and what Jesus was achieving in His death on the cross. The gospel needs to be defined because there is no longer fundamental evangelical unity on its message.

The ultimate answer to this question is Jesus Christ Himself. Jesus Christ in all the glory of His person and work *is* the gospel. He alone is the good news that the gospel proclaims against the background of our sin. The gospel that Paul preached is none

---

1. Murray, *Collected Writings*, 4:132.

other than 'Christ died for our sins according to the Scriptures … He was buried, and … rose again the third day according to the Scriptures' (1 Cor. 15:3-4). His person, His life, death and resurrection constitute the 'good news'. But before we explore further the claim that Jesus is the gospel, we need to understand why the gospel is necessary at all. To do that we must begin with creation, with the world as it came into being through the Word of God.

Beginning at the Beginning

When we turn to Genesis 1 and 2, we see that God created a world that was a theatre for His glory: 'Then God saw everything that He had made, and indeed it was very good' (Gen. 1:31). This was a world unmarred by human sin. Humanity and the rest of creation interacted without fear (Gen. 2:19-20). More importantly, however, there was no distance or doubt in the relationship between God and man. Created by direct and intimate act of God (Gen. 2:7), Adam and Eve walked in fellowship with their Creator (Gen. 3:8).

Despite this creation of a good world with true fellowship between God and Adam and Eve, this happy situation was not to continue. God had given a command to Adam, a test of his love and obedience to God. God said, 'Of every tree of the garden you may freely eat; but of the tree of the knowledge of good and evil you shall not eat, for in the day that you eat of it you shall surely die.' (Gen. 2:16-17) This was the instruction given to Adam. Bound up in this was the threat of physical and spiritual death if Adam broke the rule God had given him. Conversely a wonderful promise was implied. If Adam obeyed, eternal life would be his. The tree of life which granted everlasting life would have been his to eat from (Gen. 3:22), and he would have been confirmed forever in a state of holiness.

However, the promise of life dependent on Adam's obedience was never to be experienced. Genesis 3 tells us of the sad failure of Adam and Eve, and the consequent rupture that came into the relationship between God and His image bearers. Satan, the liar from the beginning, induced Eve to doubt the goodness of God's provision. With the false promise 'You will not surely die' (Gen. 3:4) in her right hand, she reached out, took and ate the fruit God had forbidden. In turn, Adam received the fruit from Eve and also ate. In this seemingly simple act, the first human couple rebelled against their Creator. They entered into sin by rejecting God's good commands. In succumbing to temptation, they lost the most precious thing they had, fellowship with God. Comfort and joy in God's presence was replaced with fear: 'I heard Your voice in the garden, and I was afraid because I was naked; and I hid myself' (Gen. 3:10). As Robert Candlish comments, 'the real cause of shame was not in their bodily [nakedness]… but in the guilt of their souls; and the real cause of fear was … their liability to a far more awful doom.'[2]

Understanding the Consequences

This one act of Adam had tremendous consequences for all history that followed. Some of that is outlined in Genesis 3. We are told that childbearing would now be painful (Gen. 3:16), that work would be hard (Gen. 3:17-19) and that ultimately all would experience death, for 'dust you are, and to dust you shall return' (Gen. 3:19b).

The most comprehensive account of the consequences of Adam's sin in Genesis 3 is found in Romans 5:12-19. The apostle Paul runs through the effects of the events of Genesis 3:

---

2. Robert S. Candlish, *Studies in Genesis* (Repr.; Grand Rapids: Kregel, 1979), 72-73.

ALL THINGS ARE READY

through one man [Adam] sin entered the world, and death through sin, and thus death spread to all men, because all sinned… by the one man's offence many died… the judgment which came from one offence resulted in condemnation… by the one man's offence death reigned through the one… by one man's disobedience many were made sinners.

The wreckage left by the disobedience of Adam could not be starker. Quite simply, ever since Adam's failure, 'sin reigned in death' (Rom. 5:21).

Earlier in his letter Paul had outlined the impact of this. In Romans 1:18-3:20 he explained the effects of sin on the Gentiles (who did not have God's written teaching, Rom. 1:18-31), Jews (who did have God's Word, Rom. 2:1-3:8) and then he drew his universal conclusion (Rom. 3:9-20). (His conclusion is all embracing because everyone fits into either the category of Jew or Gentile.) For the Gentiles, the picture was bleak. God had continued to clearly reveal Himself in creation, so that all who refused to honour Him were without excuse (Rom. 1:19-20). However, this knowledge of God was universally rejected and suppressed in unrighteousness (Rom 1:18b). This rejection of God was manifested in the worship of idols, 'an image made like corruptible man – and birds and four-footed animals and creeping things' (Rom. 1:23b). It was also shown in embracing sexual licence, 'the lusts of their hearts, to dishonour their bodies among themselves' (Rom. 1:24). Because of their exchange of the knowledge of God for idolatry and immorality, the world was given over to a deplorable catalogue of behaviours: 'All unrighteousness, sexual immorality, wickedness, covetousness, maliciousness; full of envy, murder, strife, deceit, evil-mindedness; *they are* whisperers, backbiters, haters of God, violent, proud, boasters, inventors of evil things, disobedient to parents, undiscerning, untrustworthy, unloving, unforgiving, unmerciful' (Rom. 1:29-31). This was where the sin of Adam had left the world, hopelessly mired in corruption, and, as such, subject to the 'wrath of God' which is 'revealed from heaven against all ungodliness and unrighteousness of men' (Rom. 1:18).

If that is the miserable place where the sin of Genesis 3 left the wider world, surely the Jews, with their privileged covenant status and the Old Testament writings, were in a better position? In Romans 2:17-24 Paul demonstrates this wasn't the case. There he discusses the Jews, those who 'know *His* will, and approve the things that are excellent, being instructed out of the law' (Rom. 2:18). Paul says of them that, however well they know God's law, inevitably and invariably they break it. As Romans 2:21-23 says, 'You, therefore, who teach another, do you not teach yourself? You who preach that a man should not steal, do you steal? You who say, "Do not commit adultery", do you commit adultery? You who abhor idols, do you rob temples? You who make your boast in the law, do you dishonour God through breaking the law?' The answer to all these rhetorical questions is, yes. Outwardly, the Jews (and all who have God's written teaching) fall short of what they know. Those who know theft is wrong themselves steal, or, if not actually stealing, they engage in coveting, or wrongfully desiring the goods of others (Rom. 7:7). Those who know sexual purity is required by the law, themselves fail to keep that standard. Again, if not failing in physical ways, they still fail in inward thoughts (Matt. 5:28). Paul is clear that the law is spiritual (Rom. 7:14); it deals with the 'thoughts and intents of the heart' (Heb. 4:12) as well as outward actions. Therefore, in thought, word and deed even those who know God's Word fail. Jews as well as Gentiles fall into the category of those who 'dishonour God through breaking the law' (Rom. 2:23).

Paul leaves us in no doubt about the universal plight of humanity. He says: 'We have previously charged both Jews and

Greeks that they are all under sin' (Rom. 3:9). Drawing on Psalm 14:1, Paul affirms that 'There is none righteous, no, not one' (Rom. 3:10). Since the fall of Adam into sin everyone in the world has been born, and lived, as unrighteous. As we are in ourselves there is no hope of restoring the right and good relationship with God that Adam originally had. Because we are sinners, we always fall short of the standard God wants. However much we try, we always fail, and so 'by the deeds of the law no flesh will be justified in His sight' (Rom. 3:20). As John Murray has said, 'for the reason that there are no doers of the law ... there is actually no justification by the works of the law.'[3]

What then? Is there no hope to regain what Adam lost? Yes, there is hope! That hope is found in the gospel of the grace of God in Jesus Christ. There is hope for each and every sinner that they can be right with God, because 'Christ Jesus came into the world to save sinners' (1 Tim. 1:15).

The Good News Promised

God was not going to leave humanity in the lost and sinful condition Adam's fall brought them into. This was revealed to Adam and Eve almost immediately. In Genesis 3:15 God said to the devil, 'And I will put enmity between you and the woman, And between your seed and her Seed; He shall bruise your head, And you shall bruise His heel.' This victory of the evil one would be overturned in his ultimate defeat. One of the children of the woman he deceived would crush his head, leading to his eternal destruction.

There are hints in Genesis 3 of what this child of the woman would have to do to win this victory. He will crush the serpent's

3. John Murray, *The Epistle to the Romans* (2 vols. in 1; London: Marshall, Morgan & Scott, 1974), 1:107.

head but his own heel will be 'bruised' (Gen. 3:15). He will suffer in victory. The nature of that suffering is hinted at in God's clothing of Adam and Eve: 'Also for Adam and his wife the Lord God made tunics of skin, and clothed them' (Gen. 3:21). The nakedness of the rebellious couple is covered. But it is covered through the death, the bloodshed of others. Animals are slain that they might benefit. This pointed to the fact that the Saviour would have to give His life to destroy the work of the devil and to bring blessing on all who believe in Him. Candlish helpfully notes, 'The covering of the nakedness of our first parents with the skins of animals, represented the way in which sin is covered, by the imputed worthiness of the great Sacrifice, the righteousness of the Lamb slain for its remission.'[4]

The whole Bible unpacks this first revelation of how the 'seed of the woman' would undo the work of Satan. Throughout the Old Testament we get clearer views of the triumph of the Saviour to come and the nature of His sufferings on behalf of His people. Many of the dealings with Abraham shed further light on the 'seed of the woman'. We find that the Saviour who would bring blessing instead of curse on many nations would descend from Abraham: 'In your seed all the nations of the earth shall be blessed' (Gen. 22:18, c.f. Gen. 12:3, 15:5, 18:18). However, for this blessing to come, again there must be suffering. The promises to Abraham were marked by the shedding of blood. In Genesis 15, these covenant promises to Abraham were sealed with the sacrifice of 'a three-year-old heifer, a three-year-old female goat, a three-year-old ram, a turtledove, and a young pigeon' (Gen. 15:9). God Himself comes and in the form of a 'a smoking oven and a burning torch' and passes through the sacrificed animals, ratifying the covenant. Blessing came through death. But ultimately

---

4. Candlish, *Genesis*, 81.

that death would need to be someone descended from Adam, rather than an animal. This is seen in God's call to Abraham to sacrifice his only son Isaac (Gen. 22:2). Of course, God spared Isaac, providing Himself a ram instead, but the message was clear: to bring ultimate blessing, a chosen son would have to die. For humanity to escape the curse of death (Gen. 2:17), the promised seed would have to die.

Further clarity was given at the time of Moses. By this time Abraham's descendants, the nation of Israel, were slaves in Egypt (as God told Abraham they would be, Gen. 15:13). But God called Moses to lead His people out of Egypt. The way God released His people from their slavery in Egypt was through the death of the Passover lamb (Exod. 12). A lamb 'without blemish, a male of the first year' (Exod. 12:5) had to die. Its blood had to be applied to the lintel and doorpost so that the angel of death would not bring the judgment of death into the house (Exod. 12:23). Freedom from slavery, and deliverance from death, was secured through the death of a spotless lamb. Delivery from spiritual slavery and death would finally arrive through the death of a spotless, that is to say sinless, individual to come.

The sacrifices established by Moses for Israel once they were free from Egypt emphasise the same truth. A priestly system was established (e.g. Exod. 28-29). The sacrifices offered under that system affirmed the need for suffering and death in order to blot out the consequences of sin. The high point of this was the Day of Atonement described in Leviticus 16. Two goats were chosen for that day. One goat was slain as a sin offering (Lev. 16:9). Having done this the high priest would 'lay both his hands on the head of the live goat, confess over it all the iniquities of the children of Israel' (Lev. 16:21). This goat would then go into the wilderness carrying away the sins of the people. Thus, in the death of the goat, and the resultant symbolic carrying away of the sins of the people '*the priest* shall make atonement for you, to cleanse you, *that* you may be clean from all your sins before the Lord' (Lev. 16:30). This priestly act of atonement introduced a key idea that the 'seed of the woman' to come must be a priest.

It was also revealed by Moses that the coming Saviour would be a prophet. The victory over Satan would be accomplished by one who would overthrow the false teaching of the serpent. In the garden Satan slyly sowed seeds of doubt about the reliability of God's Word: 'Has God indeed said?' (Gen. 3:1). He contradicted God's teaching that eating the fruit would lead to death, stating, 'You will not surely die' (Gen. 3:4). At the end of Moses' life God revealed that one was coming who would destroy the false teaching of the devil. One would be raised up who would give true teaching and to whom the people would listen. Moses said, 'The Lord your God will raise up for you a Prophet like me from your midst, from your brethren. Him you shall hear' (Deut. 18:15).

As well as being a suffering priest and a conquering prophet the Old Testament also portrays the 'seed of the woman' as a great King. This is seen most particularly in the covenant made with Israel's first faithful king, David. At the end of David's life God promised to him,

> When your days are fulfilled and you rest with your fathers, I will set up your seed after you, who will come from your body, and I will establish his kingdom... I will establish the throne of his kingdom forever. I will be his Father, and he shall be My son... your house and your kingdom shall be established forever before you. Your throne shall be established forever. (2 Sam. 7:12-16)

An everlasting kingdom was to come, with David's son at its head. The kingdom of this son is described in Psalm 72:8, 11 and 17:

He shall have dominion also from sea to sea, And from the River to the ends of the earth... Yes, all kings shall fall down before Him; All nations shall serve Him... His name shall endure forever; His name shall continue as long as the sun. And *men* shall be blessed in Him; All nations shall call Him blessed.

There was to be an all-conquering son from David's line who would fulfil the promises given to Abraham in bringing blessing to all nations. This was not to be realised in Solomon, David's heir, for, great though he was, he fell into grievous sin. And after him the story of Israel is tragically one of division and decline. But a great King would arise in time, the promised kingly branch rising in triumph from the stump of David's line (Isa. 11:1).

So, the Old Testament promised a coming 'seed of the woman,' who would suffer and yet triumph to bring good news to a world lost in sin. Much more could be said about how the Old Testament builds up the expectation of the Saviour to come. But it is now time to turn to the reality of the good news revealed in the New Testament.

The Good News Revealed and Proclaimed

Thus far we have seen that the Old Testament pointed to a suffering yet triumphing Saviour to come. The New Testament gloriously reveals the fulfilment of the Old Testament promises by announcing: 'And she will bring forth a Son, and you shall call His name Jesus, for He will save His people from their sins' (Matt. 1:21). The 'seed of the woman' had finally come, the promised good news of the gospel!

The Gospels themselves reveal who Jesus is and what He had come to do. They show us a man born of a virgin (Matt. 1:18) and who is without sin (John 8:46). They show that He

24

is indeed the prophet like Moses who was promised (Deut. 18:15), for 'He taught them as one having authority, and not as the scribes' (Matt. 7:29). They show us that He is the great King the Old Testament spoke of: 'Fear not, daughter of Zion; Behold, your King is coming, Sitting on a donkey's colt' (John 12:15). And they show us that He is the fulfilment of the Old Testament priesthood, both as the lamb of God who takes away the sin of the world (John 1:29) and as the priest who intercedes for His people (John 17). They show us that Jesus, as well as being true man (e.g. Mark 11:12), is God Himself come into the world (e.g. Matt. 1:23, 9:2, 12:8, 28:9; Mark 1:24; Luke 10:22; John 1:14, 5:18, 10:30, 14:9).

Jesus preached the good news that He was the promised Saviour, the Son of God who would die that sinners might live. From the outset of His ministry Jesus proclaimed the 'gospel of the kingdom of God ... saying, "The time is fulfilled, and the kingdom of God is at hand. Repent, and believe in the gospel"' (Mark 1:14-15). He confirmed this good news of His saving kingdom with His miracles. The curse of sin which had brought disease and disfigurement into God's good creation (Rom. 8:22) was visibly reversed in Jesus' miracles – the blind being given sight, the deaf having hearing restored, the lame walking. All this is confirmation of the good news Jesus came to preach (Luke 7:22).

Jesus' gospel preaching was centred on Himself, yet it was not a selfish message. He called those who were weary and heavy laden over sin to come to *Him* for rest (Matt. 11:28). He told those who were thirsty to come to *Him* for drink (John 7:37). When asked the way to heaven, Jesus answered, 'I am the way, the truth, and the life. No one comes to the Father except through Me' (John 14:6). Similarly, He stated, 'I am the door. If anyone enters by Me, he will be saved' (John 10:9). Again, Jesus was clear that only He could undo the curse of death:

'I am the resurrection and the life. He who believes in Me, though he may die, he shall live' (John 11:25). The good news of heaven regained, of the restoration of eternal fellowship with God that Adam lost – that good news, Jesus said, was found only in Himself.

That good news, however, only came through Jesus' suffering and death. The pivotal moment in Matthew's Gospel is Peter's confession: 'You are the Christ, the Son of the living God' (Matt. 16:16). Following this we read, 'From that time Jesus began to show to His disciples that He must go to Jerusalem, and suffer many things from the elders and chief priests and scribes, and be killed, and be raised the third day.' (Matt. 16:21) The good news that Jesus was preaching – heaven, fellowship with God, freedom from condemnation due to sin and the offer of Himself as our Saviour – all this was only possible through Jesus' suffering. Jesus took upon Himself the curse of our sin in death, destroying the power of death, and rising triumphant. He voluntarily did this for us and therefore said, 'I am the good shepherd. The good shepherd gives His life for the sheep' (John 10:11). The giving of His life was a bitter thing. He who knew unbroken fellowship in light for all eternity with His Father would be clouded in fearful darkness and left to cry in desolation, 'My God, My God, why have You forsaken Me?' (Matt. 27:46). And yet, Jesus did this. He died that others might have life. He lovingly took the punishment of death for sin, that sinners might know eternal life. The good news is Jesus Himself: God becoming man, and doing all this to bring salvation.

The New Testament unfolds and develops the truths of the gospel narratives so that we might appreciate the power of the gospel. Having been commissioned to 'Go into all the world and preach the gospel to every creature' (Mark 16:15) the Church did just that. The message that Peter took out into the world was simply this: 'the good news of peace through Jesus Christ, who is Lord of all' (Acts 10:36, NIV). Paul similarly proclaimed that 'through this Man [Jesus] is preached to you the forgiveness of sins' (Acts 13:38). The message of the Church was focused on Jesus: 'I determined not to know anything among you except Jesus Christ and Him crucified' (1 Cor. 2:2, c.f. Phil. 1:21, 1 Pet. 2:7). The good news the Church preached was the good news of Jesus, that God 'made Him who knew no sin *to be* sin for us, that we might become the righteousness of God in Him' (2 Cor. 5:21).

Paul pressed home the contrast between the failure of Adam, and the salvation that there is in Jesus, in Romans 5. Earlier we saw how Paul demonstrated the universal effect of Adam's sin. However, Paul also showed how Adam's sin is dealt with in Christ. He states: 'if by the one man's offence many died, much more the grace of God and the gift by the grace of the one Man, Jesus Christ, abounded to many.' (Rom. 5:15) In and through what Jesus has done, the righteousness that Adam lost is given back as a gift. Indeed, Christ's righteousness exceeds Adam's, for He was faithful to death, even when suffering the curse for sin.

The gospel message is ultimately a plea for sinners ruined in Adam to receive, through trust in what Jesus has done for them, a new, reconciled status. The gospel is clear: 'By one man's disobedience many were made sinners, so also by one Man's obedience many will be made righteous' (Rom. 5:19). The challenge of the gospel is: are we those who are made righteous in Christ, trusting in His life, death and resurrection to take away our sins, or are we still lost in the sin that Adam plunged us into? The plea, the universal invitation of the gospel is this: believe in Jesus and come to know the righteousness that there is in Him!

2

GOD'S SOVEREIGNTY
IN THE GOSPEL

*You pray for the conversion of others. In what terms, now, do
you intercede for them? … I think that what you do is pray in
categorical terms that God will, quite simply and decisively,
save them: that He will open the eyes of their understanding,
soften their hard hearts … and move their wills to receive the
Saviour… When you pray for unconverted people, you do so on
the assumption that it is in God's power to bring them to faith.*
J. I. Packer (1926-2020)[1]

The gospel outlined in chapter 1 is good news. But it is often not
received as such. This raises the question, why? If God has gone
to such lengths to procure good news for sinners, even to the
extent of becoming man, enduring the mockery and rejection
of His own creatures and giving His life on Calvary, why does
not everyone accept the gospel? Does God not have the ability,
the power, to ensure all rejoice in the gospel which is 'worthy
of all acceptance' (1 Tim. 1:15)? To answer these questions, we
first of all need to consider the glorious being of our triune God
and secondly, within this setting, the sovereignty of God.

---

1. *Evangelism and the Sovereignty of God* (London: InterVarsity
Fellowship, 1961), 15.

Who Is Our God?

God is not just a bigger, more powerful version of ourselves. Yes, we are made in the image of God (Gen. 1:26-27), but that does not mean God is just like us only better. God is greater than we can imagine. We are made in His image, but we do not define who God is. He is beyond our fathoming: 'Who can fathom the Spirit of the LORD, or instruct the LORD as his counsellor?' (Isa. 40:13, NIV). We cannot grasp or understand the depths of God. He is beyond us. In the words of Heinrich Bullinger, 'the eternal, excellent, and mighty God is greater than all majesty, and than all the eloquence of all men.'[2]

This 'incomprehensibility' of God can be seen in what are called His incommunicable attributes. These are things which are true of God, but are not and cannot be true of us due to our creaturely finiteness. His triune nature as Father, Son and Holy Spirit is a primary example. Only regarding God can it be said 'in the unity of the Godhead there be three persons, of one substance, power, and eternity; God the Father, God the Son, and God the Holy Ghost' (*Westminster Confession of Faith* 2:3). Also, there are many attributes which set God apart. One instance of this is His self-existence. We simply read: 'In the beginning God created' (Gen 1:1). God has always been. By contrast we are created, we are those who have been 'knitted together' (Ps. 139:13, NIV). God, however, simply is. He is the eternal 'I AM' (Exod. 3:14). There is nothing before Him, and there can be nothing after Him: 'I *am* the First and I *am* the Last; Besides Me *there is* no God' (Isa. 44:6). Accordingly, we confess, 'Even from everlasting to everlasting, You *are* God' (Ps. 90:2).

---

2. Heinrich Bullinger, *The Decades of Heinrich Bullinger* (2 vols.; repr.; Grand Rapids: Reformation Heritage Books, 2004), 2:173.

Because God simply is, He exists independently of time and is not constrained by it. We are told this in Psalm 90:4: 'For a thousand years in Your sight *Are* like yesterday when it is past, And *like* a watch in the night.' We are creatures of time, and so continually we need to be told: 'Beloved, do not forget this one thing, that with the Lord one day is as a thousand years' (2 Pet. 3:8). We are prone to make God like us in respect of time, as in other ways, but the Bible tells us this is not so. God is eternal, He is radically 'other' than we are. We experience succession, time going past, with the change and development that entails, but God exists outside of time as 'the High and Lofty One Who inhabits eternity' (Isa. 57:15). While all in this world changes and decays, this is not true of God, for 'You *are* the same, And Your years will have no end' (Ps. 102:27).

This acknowledgment that God is the self-existent I AM, the one who is outside of time, carries some important consequences. Once we realise that God is beyond being constrained by time, we can move on to see that God is not constrained by space, for 'heaven and the heaven of heavens cannot contain You' (1 Kings 8:27). This means that God is not located in one place but is everywhere, and so Psalm 139 asks, 'Where can I go from Your Spirit? Or where can I flee from Your presence?' and answers, 'If I ascend into heaven, You *are* there; If I make my bed in hell, behold, You *are there*. *If* I take the wings of the morning, *And* dwell in the uttermost parts of the sea, Even there Your hand shall lead me, And Your right hand shall hold me' (Ps. 139:7-10). The God who is outside of time, is still everywhere present in time.

Exploring still further, the eternal God, who is everywhere, knows all things. Nothing that occurs in time can add to His knowledge or surprise Him. It is God alone who can say, 'For I *am* God, and *there is* no other; *I am* God, and *there is* none like

Me, Declaring the end from the beginning, And from ancient times *things* that are not *yet* done' (Isa. 46:9-10). We learn, we grow in understanding. How things will fall out are unknown to us from the mundane, 'Will my sports team win?' to the life changing, 'Will she say yes and marry me?' But not so with God: 'Known to God from eternity are all His works' (Acts 15:18). Everything that will happen in the future is as clear to God, as what happened yesterday is to us. Before our God we have to simply bow and say, 'Great is our Lord, and mighty in power; His understanding is infinite' (Ps. 147:5).

If God knows all things, if He is everywhere present, and if He is outside of time, what does that mean? Well, it means something else that sets God apart from us – He is unchangeable. We change all the time. While remaining the same essential person, we grow, we mature, new information comes to us, changing our decisions and our likes and dislikes. But God is not like this. He is constant in who He is. As someone who knows everything and who is eternally outside of time there is nothing that can cause Him to grow or develop. This is clearly taught in Psalm 102:25-27 where God is contrasted with what might seem permanent and immovable to us, the very world and universe. The creation, 'the foundations of the earth, and the heavens' are from God. They are 'the work of your hands.' However, as great as they are, they are unlike God, because, 'They will perish, but you endure.' The same truth of the unchangeableness of God is taught in Malachi 3:6: 'For I *am* the Lord, I do not change; Therefore you are not consumed, O sons of Jacob.' And again, in James 1:17, God is spoken of as 'the Father of lights, with whom there is no variation or shadow of turning.'

This does not of course imply that God is frozen, static, or some sort of stone statue. God is life, and life abundant. He dwells in unbroken triune fellowship and glory. Proverbs 8 gives us an insight into this where the relationship between the Father and Son is described: 'I was daily *His* delight, Rejoicing always before Him' (Prov. 8:30). God's life is one of constant delight and joy. He is the opposite of a deaf, blind, mute idol (Ps. 115:4-7). Nor does it mean He is remote from us, for in trouble He is our ever-present help (Ps. 46:1). Yet it does mean God's character is fixed, His purposes are unchanged and unchangeable. As Thomas Boston has said, God 'is the same in all his perfections, constant to his intentions, steady to his purpose, unchangeably fixed and persevering in all his decrees and resolutions.'[3] That is a great comfort. In all that He is, our God is the same yesterday, today and forever.

God, then, is very different to us. He is uncreated, eternal, everywhere present, all knowing and unchangeable. God is all of these things and more (His other 'communicable' attributes include wisdom, power, holiness, justice, goodness and love) undividedly and entirely. Since God is a Spirit (John 4:24) He is not made up of various things. He isn't composed of a bit of eternity, knowledge and other attributes which together make God. Rather, He is all that He is all the time. God in all His acts never ceases to be love (1 John 4:8), light (1 John 1:5), just and holy (Heb. 12:29). All God's attributes are a perfect unity, an inseparable harmony, making Him the glorious Triune God we worship.

God Is Sovereign in All Things

This is the wonder (in part) of who our God is. One of the ways God manifests the glory of who He is, is in His sovereignty over all things. In a sense this simply flows from His being the Creator. He spoke and all the universe came into being

---

3.   Thomas Boston, *The Complete Works of Thomas Boston* (ed. Samuel M'Millan; 12 vols.; London: William Tegg and Co., 1854), 1:83.

(Gen. 1). Because He is the creative power behind the cosmos: because all owes its being to Him, then by definition He rules and reigns over His creation. John Murray captures this well, 'to say that God is sovereign is but to affirm that God is One, and that God is God.'[4]

Jeremiah 18 give us an image to explain this. God directed Jeremiah to go to a potter's house and watch the potter working on the clay. As he saw the potter working Jeremiah's attention was directed to the power the potter had over the clay. He could mould it into any shape he desired, and if the shaping went wrong, he could simply start over again (Jer. 18:4). This, God said to Jeremiah is just my relation of sovereignty to the world as its Creator: 'Can I not do with you as this potter has done? declares the Lord. Behold, like the clay in the potter's hand, so are you in my hand' (Jer. 18:6, ESV). Philip Ryken explains this passage as follows: 'God can do whatever he wants with you. This is what it means for him to be God... In his hands rest all power, rule, control, authority, kingdom, government and dominion.'[5]

But God's sovereignty isn't simply something we deduce from His position as Creator. It is positively declared in the Bible again and again. In Genesis 14:19-20, God is acknowledged as the 'possessor of heaven and earth,' the one who as 'God Most High' is sovereign over all His people's enemies. The God who comes to covenant with Abraham in Genesis 17:1 is *El Shaddai*, 'Almighty God.' This God who specially cares for and blesses Abraham's descendants in the Old Testament, the nation of Israel, never for one moment relinquishes His claim to universal sovereignty and dominion. For, as Moses declares, 'Heaven and

---

4. Murray, *Collected Writings*, 4:191.
5. Philip Graham Ryken, *Jeremiah and Lamentations: From Sorrow to Hope* (Wheaton: Crossway, 2001), 294.

the highest heavens belong to the Lord your God, *also* the earth with all that *is* in it' (Deut. 10:14).

The great truths of God's sovereignty find expression in the praises of Israel. David rejoices that 'Yours, O Lord, *is* the greatness, The power and the glory, The victory and the majesty; For all *that is* in heaven and in earth *is Yours;* Yours *is* the kingdom, O Lord, And You are exalted as head over all' (1 Chron. 29:11). God is the 'great King over all the earth' (Ps. 47:2) whose reign should give gladness to the earth (Ps. 97:1). Psalm 115:3 (NIV) declares: 'Our God is in heaven; he does whatever pleases him.' The same thought is expressed in Psalm 135:6: 'Whatever the Lord pleases He does, In heaven and in earth, In the seas and in all deep places.' God's people rejoice that 'Your dominion *endures* throughout all generations' (Ps. 145:13).

No less do the prophets declare the same truth. Just think of Isaiah 40. God's people are summoned, Isaiah 40:9, to 'Behold your God!' What is the God they are to behold like? He is the God who holds all the waters of the world 'in the hollow of His hand,' who 'measured heaven with the width of His hand' and who weighs 'the mountains in scales, And the hills in a balance' (Isa. 40:12). Before him, 'the nations *are* as a drop in a bucket' (Isa. 40:15). Indeed, 'All nations before Him *are* as nothing, And they are counted by Him less than nothing and worthless' (Isa. 40:17).

What is the implication of this? Simply, as Isaiah unfolds for us, that the Lord reigns over the cosmos and all its inhabitants:

Have you not known? Have you not heard? Has it not been told you from the beginning? Have you not understood from the foundations of the earth? *It is* He who sits above the circle of the earth, And its inhabitants *are* like grasshoppers, Who stretches out the heavens like a curtain, And spreads them out like a tent to dwell in. He brings the princes to nothing; He makes the judges of the earth useless (Isa. 40:21-23).

Nor does this sovereign ruling over the world in any way exhaust God's resources, for 'The everlasting God, the Lord, The Creator of the ends of the earth, Neither faints nor is weary. His understanding is unsearchable' (Isa. 40:28). In the exercise of this unlimited sovereign power, God needs no help. His infinite, unsearchable understanding is sufficient to determine how He should act in sovereign power: 'Who has directed the Spirit of the Lord, Or *as* His counsellor has taught Him? With whom did He take counsel, and *who* instructed Him, And taught Him in the path of justice? Who taught Him knowledge, And showed Him the way of understanding?' (Isa. 40:13-14). The sovereign God truly can say, 'My counsel shall stand, And I will do all My pleasure' (Isa. 46:10). Before this great God, we have to acknowledge our impotence. Only He can say, 'I work, and who will reverse it?' (Isa. 43:13).

Other Old Testament prophets outline God's sovereignty in a similar way to Isaiah. Jeremiah places even the sufferings of Israel under the sovereign control of God: 'Who *is* he *who* speaks and it comes to pass, *When* the Lord has not commanded *it*? *Is it* not from the mouth of the Most High That woe and well-being proceed? Why should a living man complain, A man for the punishment of his sins?' (Lam. 3:37-39). And Daniel summarises well the whole Old Testament prophetic teaching on God's sovereignty: 'He does according to His will in the army of heaven, And *among* the inhabitants of the earth. No one can restrain His hand, Or say to Him, What have You done?' (Dan. 4:35).

This same picture of the Lord's sovereign power continues in the New Testament. The Lord's prayer portrays God as the one on whom all depend for their daily bread (Matt. 6:11). Jesus teaches that even the death of a seemingly insignificant bird is under the sovereign disposing of God's will: 'Are not two sparrows sold for a copper coin? And not one of them falls to the ground apart from your Father's will' (Matt. 10:29). All things, Jesus declares, are possible with God (Matt. 19:26, c.f. Luke 1:37). Paul proclaims that God 'works all things according to the counsel of His will' (Eph. 1:11). He preached to the Athenians that God 'made from one blood every nation of men to dwell on all the face of the earth, and has determined their pre-appointed times and the boundaries of their dwellings' (Acts. 17:26). God is still the sovereign King, 'the blessed and only Potentate, the King of kings and Lord of lords' (1 Tim. 6:15). Fittingly, the final book of the Bible, Revelation, is clear that the great sweep of history is under God's direction and control. One key message of that book is 'Alleluia! For the Lord God Omnipotent reigns!' (Rev. 19:6).

God's sovereignty manifests itself in His sustaining and upholding the existence of all creation, 'For You created all things, And by Your will they exist and were created' (Rev. 4:11). Because God is 'before all things' it is true that 'in Him all things consist' and all things are 'for Him' (Col. 1:16-17). This sovereignty is comforting for God's people because it assures them all things, even their sufferings (1 Pet. 3:17), are ordained by God to 'work for good' (Rom. 8:28). God's sovereignty also reminds us of our utter dependence on God. Everything in life is only accomplished 'by the will of God' (Rom. 12:32). Instead of saying we will do this or that we need to say, in recognition of God's sovereignty, 'if the Lord wills, we shall live and do this or that' (James. 4:15). We bow before the sovereign God.

God Is Sovereign in Salvation

From Genesis to Revelation God is declared to be sovereign. This general sovereignty of God is manifested in a particular way in salvation, namely, it is God who determines who will be saved. As we are told by Jesus, 'many are called but few *are* chosen' (Matt. 22:14).

God's choice of His people is taught throughout the Old Testament. Abraham did not choose God. God chose him from the darkness of sin and idolatry. We are told that 'Your fathers, *including* Terah, the father of Abraham and the father of Nahor, dwelt on the other side of the River in old times; and they served other gods' (Josh. 24:2). It was not Abraham who sought God, it was God who came to Abraham and promised unilaterally to him, 'I will make you a great nation; I will bless you And make your name great; And you shall be a blessing' (Gen. 12:2). God's initiative in choosing who would be His continued within Abraham's family. When twins were to be born to Abraham's son Isaac, God came to Isaac's wife Rebekah and said, 'Two nations *are* in your womb, Two peoples shall be separated from your body; *One* people shall be stronger than the other, And the older shall serve the younger' (Gen. 25:23). In a reversal of the natural order, Jacob, the younger son, was God's chosen and Esau, the older, was to be rejected. This was God's sovereign choice, against the cultural expectation of the time that the older son inherits the blessing. Because of the sovereign action of God in choosing Abraham, then again in choosing his grandson Jacob (later called Israel), Moses could say, 'The Lord did not set his affection on you and choose you because you were more numerous than other peoples, for you were the fewest of all peoples'. (Deut. 7:7 NIV) God's chosen people Israel were unconditionally favoured by God. They were not, in themselves, worthy of being a special people. They did not have more faith or good works than other people. Rather 'the Lord your God has chosen you to be a people for Himself, a special treasure … because the Lord loves you, and because He would keep the oath which He swore to your fathers' (Deut.

7:6-8). Israel's existence as a saved people (Exod. 20:1) was due to nothing other than the sovereign good pleasure of God. As Calvin remarked, 'Moses takes it for granted, that there was nothing naturally in the people to cause their condition to be better or more distinguished; and hence infers, that there was no other reason why God should choose them, except His mere choice of them.'[6]

This teaching that God's people – those who believe and accept the gospel – are chosen, or elected, by God is equally clear in the New Testament. Before exploring this, it is worth pausing to consider that salvation in Jesus had always been God's plan and purpose.

God knew and ordained that salvation would be necessary because of sin, and that He would bring about that salvation. Jesus is described as 'the Lamb slain from the foundation of the world' (Rev. 13:8). Before the world came into being God purposed that His Son would come as the once for all sacrifice for sin, and in so doing would 'save his people from their sins' (Matt. 1:21). Jesus Himself, as He stands before Pilate, reminds His apparent judge that Pilate only had power because it was the will of the Father: 'Jesus answered, You could have no power at all against Me unless it had been given you from above' (John 19:11). God's eternal purpose was always that His Son would lay down His life as a ransom for many captives (Mark 10:45), and in His final days Jesus was deeply conscious of this. The apostles, too, as they preached the gospel message, proclaimed the same truth. They knew that 'truly against Your holy Servant Jesus, whom You anointed, both Herod and Pontius Pilate, with the Gentiles and the people of Israel, were gathered together to do whatever Your hand and Your purpose determined before to be done' (Acts 4:27-28). The very act of Jesus' priestly, sacrificial

---

6.   Calvin, *Calvin's Commentaries*, 2:356.

death, was the result of God's purpose and determination, and was not simply the doing of wicked men.

However, not only does the New Testament teach that salvation through the death and resurrection of Jesus was always God's purpose. It also teaches, just like the Old Testament, that the fruit of that death – the salvation of individuals – is predestined by God. God has a chosen people that He will save through Jesus' death. It is the undoubted testimony of Jesus and His apostles that 'You did not choose Me, but I chose you' (John 15:16).

This is expressed clearly in Paul's letter to the Ephesians. God, Paul declares, 'chose us in Him before the foundation of the world' (Eph. 1:4). Before the world came into being, God had His chosen people whom He would save in Christ. This could not be on the basis of anything done in time, because the choice was prior to the existence of the cosmos. Indeed, Paul explicitly says that God 'predestined us to adoption as sons by Jesus Christ to Himself, according to the good pleasure of His will' (Eph. 1:5).

Paul excludes our goodness or faith or choice from God's predestinating choice, so that salvation might be to the 'praise of the glory of His grace' (Eph. 1:6). Our inheritance, our legacy of a life with the triune God in glory forever, is not because of our wisdom, but because we have been 'predestined according to the purpose of Him who works all things according to the counsel of His will' (Eph. 1:11). This has to be so, because by nature, due to the fall in Adam, all are 'dead in trespasses and sins' and only the sovereign predestinating power of God can make 'alive' (Eph. 2:1, 5). Because salvation is due to the sovereign choice of God we can confess:

> For by grace you have been saved through faith, and that not
> of yourselves; *it is* the gift of God, not of works, lest anyone
> should boast. For we are His workmanship, created in Christ

Jesus for good works, which God prepared beforehand that we should walk in them (Eph. 2:8-10).

So, for Paul, salvation is as a result of God's 'eternal purpose which He accomplished in Christ Jesus our Lord' (Eph. 3:11). It is all of God's grace, not of our foreseen works, for God 'has saved us and called us with a holy calling, not according to our works, but according to His own purpose and grace which was given to us in Christ Jesus before time began' (2 Tim. 1:9). The rest of the New Testament also ascribes salvation, not to our choice of God, but to God's choice of us, for when we are born again we are 'born, not of blood, nor of the will of the flesh, nor of the will of man, but of God' (John 1:13). As a result of this, it is always the case that, 'as many as had been appointed to eternal life believed' (Acts 13:48). The scriptural testimony is, in the words of Louis Berkhof, that there is 'an eternal act of God whereby He, in sovereign good pleasure, and on account of no foreseen merit in them, chooses a certain number ... to be the recipients of special grace and of eternal salvation.'[7]

Salvation, then, is first due to God's predestination, His electing grace. This carries with it a negative corollary. Those who are not saved have in consequence been passed over by God. By definition if some are chosen for salvation, there are others who have not been chosen to salvation, and are therefore left to condemnation. As W. G. T. Shedd said, 'If God does not elect a person, he rejects him. If God decides not to convert a sinner into a saint, he decides to let him remain a sinner.'[8] This difficult truth is most clearly presented to us in Romans 9. Paul, in considering Israel's rejection of their Messiah, dwells on God's choice of Jacob rather than his older twin brother

---

7. Louis Berkhof, *Systematic Theology* (Grand Rapids: Eerdmans, 1996), 114.

8. W.G.T. Shedd, *Dogmatic Theology* (3rd edition; Ed. Alan W. Gomes; Phillipsburg: P&R Publishing, 2003), 333.

Esau to inherit the covenant blessing (Gen. 25:23). Abraham had been given the covenant promise that 'In your seed all the nations of the earth shall be blessed' (Gen. 22:18). God chose for that blessing (ultimately found in Jesus Christ) to come through Jacob and his descendants and not Esau. Paul argues, following the reasoning of Malachi chapter 1, that choosing Jacob as the seed through whom the world would be blessed inevitably involved as its counterpart the rejection of Esau, that is, the promise would not be fulfilled through him. Just as Jacob was 'loved' (chosen to inherit the promises) so Esau was 'hated' (not chosen to receive the promises). On neither account, Paul says, was this because of works that they had done, but simply that God's sovereign purposes might have their way (Rom. 9:13). Specifically, the rejection of Esau was not because he was a worse person than Jacob: '(for *the children* not yet being born, nor having done any good or evil, that the purpose of God according to election might stand, not of works but of Him who calls), it was said to her, "The older shall serve the younger"' (Rom. 9:11-12). What we have here is 'a declaration of the sovereign counsel of God as it is concerned with the ultimate destinies of men' apart from their works.[9]

Now Paul is aware how difficult this teaching is to accept. He immediately realises that God deciding not to save some might leave us with the view that God is harsh and unfair. But he refuses to accept that deduction. None of us, Paul says, deserve the saving mercy of God. We are all sinners. We are all part of that 'lump' of fallen sinful humanity (Rom. 9:21). We are all those on whom the wrath of God abides (John 3:36, KJV) and are under condemnation because our deeds are evil (John 3:19). As John Murray notes, 'Paul is ... now dealing with God's sovereign rights ... over man as sinners.'[10]

---

9. Murray, *Romans*, 2:24.
10. Murray, *Romans*, 2:32.

Therefore, it is a positive choice in God to show any mercy. If He passes over some, and doesn't show them saving mercy, that is not unrighteous, for none deserve salvation. It is simply a fact, given we are sinners, that it is God's prerogative to say, 'I will have mercy on whomever I will have mercy, and I will have compassion on whomever I will have compassion' (Rom. 9:15). Moving on from Jacob and Esau, Paul uses the example of Pharaoh as a case study of why God passes over some in not showing them saving mercy. Pharaoh hardened his heart against God, and God gave him over to the hardness of his heart. Why? That God's power in crushing His enemies might be seen: 'For this very purpose I have raised you up, that I may show My power in you, and that My name may be declared in all the earth' (Rom. 9:17).

Still, it might be thought this is unfair. What hope did Pharaoh have, as he could never resist the sovereign will of God? Paul gives two further responses. He first reminds us of our place before God. We are creatures, He is the Creator. If God refuses to extend mercy to some sinners like Pharaoh, that is His unalienable right: 'Does not the potter have power over the clay, from the same lump to make one vessel for honour and another for dishonour?' (Rom. 9:21, c.f. Isa. 45:9). If God leaves Pharaoh to his sins, as our maker, He has that right. Paul's second response builds on this. He says, while God shows His holy anger against sin in leaving some to be condemned, He does not leave those like Pharaoh without any mercy or opportunity to repent. God 'endures with much longsuffering the vessels of wrath prepared for destruction' (Rom. 9:22).

Yes, God has chosen not to save some like Pharaoh. But they still are recipients of God's 'longsuffering'. As Shedd notes, 'In this divine self-restraint, God evidences kindness even toward those whose obstinate self-determination to sin he does not think proper to overcome by special grace.'[11] That longsuffering ought to have the positive effect of leading sinners to repentance. The question is posed in Romans 2:4: 'Do you despise the riches of His goodness, forbearance, and longsuffering, not knowing that the goodness of God leads you to repentance?' In the case of Pharaoh, and others, the answer is yes. While God's goodness to them should have led them to repentance, they despised it. So, while God has sovereignly decreed not to save them, their condemnation is not 'unfair'. They themselves despise the 'longsuffering' shown to them, which if embraced would lead to their salvation, so, as Shedd asks, 'what ground for complaint have they before the bar of eternal justice?'[12]

Conclusion

To recap, why are all not saved? The answer lies partly in the human heart. Sin has not only corrupted us, destroyed our fellowship with God and brought us under just condemnation, but it has made us twisted and perverse. There is no greater perversity than to refuse Jesus Christ in the gospel of redeeming grace. To the sinner, Jesus is as a root out of dry ground, having no form or comeliness that we should desire Him (Isa. 53:2). Only grace can show us the beauty of Jesus as the one who is 'altogether lovely' (Song. 5:16). However, the answer also lies in the inscrutable sovereignty of God. The mystery of the divine will does not yield to human reasoning. Why God justly condemns some and in inexplicable grace saves others is beyond our finite, sinful minds, as we might expect, given the nature of God delineated in this chapter. God's ways are higher than

---

11. W. G. T. Shedd, *Critical and Doctrinal Commentary on Romans* (Repr.; Minneapolis: Klock & Klock, 1978), 299.

12. Shedd, *Romans*, 298.

our ways, as is His very being, and His thoughts higher than our thoughts. The ways of God will always leave us exclaiming:

> Oh, the depth of the riches both of the wisdom and knowledge of God! How unsearchable *are* His judgments and His ways past finding out! 'For who has known the mind of the Lord? Or who has become His counsellor?' 'Or who has first given to Him And it shall be repaid to him?' For of Him and through Him and to Him *are* all things, to whom *be* glory forever. Amen (Rom. 11:33-36).

3

WHAT IS THE GOSPEL OFFER?

It is ordinary for a man to beg from God, for we are but His
beggars; but it is a miracle to see God beg at man. Yet here is the
Potter begging from the clay; the Saviour seeking from sinners.
Samuel Rutherford (1600-1661)[1]

While God is sovereign in salvation (He has predestined some
to salvation and passed by others) it is equally clear that the good
news of the gospel is for all. The Church is to 'Go therefore and
make disciples of all the nations, baptising them in the name of
the Father and of the Son and of the Holy Spirit' (Matt. 28:19).
The gospel is to be proclaimed throughout the world. But when
we talk of offering the gospel, what do we have in mind? Is the
preaching of the gospel an invitation, a command, a promise?
We will see that it is all of these and more.

The Gospel as an Invitation

Imagine the excitement at the announcement of a royal
wedding. The media are full of discussions and descriptions
of the event. Nothing will be lacking. The wedding ceremony

---

1. Samuel Rutherford, *Fourteen Communion Sermons* (Glasgow: Charles
   Glass & Co., 1877), 254.

will be glorious, full of sparkling beauty, pomp and pageantry. The meal will be the finest feast of culinary fare, exquisitely presented. The lavish evening celebrations will be memorable. Then imagine one day as you look through the post a lavishly embossed letter is there. Wonder of wonders – you have an invitation from the King to attend! What exciting news. All would be set aside to attend and be at the centre of such a magnificent occasion.

Well, Jesus says that this is exactly what the gospel is – an invitation to a royal feast. This is the image we are given in the parable in Matthew 22:1-14 (and the parallel passage in Luke 14:15-24). Here Jesus tells us the good news of the gospel is like 'a king who gave a wedding feast for his son' (Matt. 22:2, ESV). Just as in preparation for any other wedding feast, there were invitations to be given out. And so, the King 'sent out his servants to call those who were invited to the wedding' (Matt. 22:3). In context, this picture is the invitation to the Jews to believe in their long-promised Messiah now come into the world. It is an invitation to see Jesus as God's servant, the one in whom God delighted and on whom was the Spirit of God (Isa. 42:1). But the parable takes an unexpected turn: those invited 'were not willing to come' (Matt. 22:3). How surprising that a royal wedding invitation would be refused out of hand! However, this is exactly what happened. Jesus came to His own, but they did not receive Him (John 1:11).

The parable continues with another surprise. The King, far from immediately rejecting those who turned down his invitation, invites them again, and increases the earnestness of the invitation by describing the glory of the wedding feast: 'Tell those who are invited, "See, I have prepared my dinner; my oxen and fatted cattle *are* killed, and all things *are* ready. Come to the wedding"' (Matt. 22:4). There was no reason for the rejection of the invitation. Everything expected at a royal wedding was there and ready. The feasting would be great! With this assurance, and additional motive to accept, the invitation goes forth again, 'Come'. This was a way of saying to Israel, that nothing was lacking in Jesus. He truly was the glorious all sufficient prophet, priest and king that the Old Testament promised. He has power to forgive sin (Luke 7:48) and grant eternal life (John 11:25). Because of who He was (and is), the invitation to the wedding feast is 'worthy of all acceptance' (1 Tim. 1:15).

Despite this plea, those invited continue to spurn the invitation (Matt. 22:5), and some went further, seizing and killing the messengers who brought the King's invitation (Matt. 22:6). This is a clear reference to the Jews who, over generations, had 'killed the prophets' (Luke 11:47) and who would soon cry regarding Jesus Himself, 'crucify him, crucify him' (Luke 23:21). In the face of such provocation, the King's patience comes to an end: 'But when the king heard *about it,* he was furious. And he sent out his armies, destroyed those murderers, and burned up their city' (Matt. 22:7). The destruction of Jerusalem in AD 70 is a direct consequence of Israel's continued refusal to accept God's invitations to receive His Son. The gospel is a divine invitation, but its refusal carries serious consequences.

However, there was still a royal wedding, and there needed to be guests. And so, the invitation that there was a feast and that 'all things *are* ready' now went out more widely: 'Therefore go into the highways, and as many as you find, invite to the wedding' (Matt. 22:9). Accordingly, the invitation went out until 'the wedding *hall* was filled with guests' (Matt. 22:10). Similarly, the invitation to come to Jesus will go throughout all the world until all God's people are saved and ready for 'the marriage supper of the Lamb' (Rev. 19:9).

Luke's account gives us more colour. The servants are told to 'Go out quickly into the streets and lanes of the city, and bring in here *the* poor and *the* maimed and *the* lame and *the* blind.' (Luke 14:21). After these came, we are told 'still there is room' (Luke 14:22). As a result, the invitation goes 'out into the highways and hedges' with the instruction 'compel *them* to come in, that my house may be filled' (Luke 14:23). What we have highlighted are the unworthiness of the guests for so great a feast and the great urgency of accepting the invitation. Who is invited to royal weddings? Those who are 'the great and the good'. Those who have a worthiness either through family connection, wealth or some great contribution to civic society. But here, for this royal wedding, the invites go to those with no worthiness, the outcasts of society. This picture is designed to show that we need no merit of our own to earn the gospel invitation. We receive the invitation and accept it in our need, not in any supposed worthiness. As James Durham has said the invitation is 'to great and small, rich and poor, learned and unlearned, gracious and graceless, hypocrites and profane. There is here no exception of persons with Him; the blessed God is content to match with the most graceless and godless'.[2]

We are strongly encouraged to accept the invitation. There is a drive to have it accepted. Those giving the invitation are to 'compel' those receiving it to accept. There is an urgency. The wedding feast is ready; it must be fully attended. This is the note of the gospel as well. It must be accepted. As James Durham again said:

> Christ the Bridegroom and His Father are very willing to have the match made up and the marriage completed. Therefore He sends forth His servants with a strict commission, not only to tell sinners that all things are ready, and to invite them, but

---

2.   James Durham, *The Unsearchable Riches of Christ* (Repr.; Morgan, PA: Soli Deo Gloria. 2002), 62.

to compel them (as Luke has it in 14:23), to come in; to stir them up, and press them to it.[3]

Another wonderful example of the gospel as an invitation is found in Matthew 11:28, where Jesus invites all to come to Himself: 'Come to Me, all *you* who labour and are heavy laden, and I will give you rest.' The context is Jesus rejoicing in His Father's sovereignty. He has just pronounced judgment on impenitent Chorazin and Bethsaida (Matt. 11:20-24) and acknowledged that this is the will of God as a just desert of their sin: 'I thank You, Father, Lord of heaven and earth, that You have hidden these things from *the* wise and prudent and have revealed them to babes. Even so, Father, for so it seemed good in Your sight.' (Matt. 11:25-26). Further, Jesus proclaimed that only those 'to whom the Son wills to reveal *Him*' would savingly know the Father (Matt. 11:27). Those brought in to the family of God are those chosen by the Son, they are those He discloses Himself to in such a way as bring them to believe in Him. But, perhaps conscious of the wrong inferences that can be drawn from God's sovereignty, Jesus immediately moves on to invite all to come to Him. The sovereign will of God, Father, Son and Holy Spirit in no way hinders the gracious loving invitation to all: 'Come to Me, all *you* who labour and are heavy laden, and I will give you rest.'

This invitation is to come to Jesus. Jesus is the gospel; He is the good news. So, it is right that gospel invitations are centred on coming to Jesus. The recipients are those who are in need. Those Jesus invites are 'weary and burdened' (NIV); they are struggling with the trials of this life. (Who doesn't struggle with life in a fallen world?) To them the gospel comes in the person of Jesus and says, 'I will give you rest.' I will give you rest from the condemnation of sin, as my blood cleanses from

---

3. Durham, *Unsearchable Riches*, 55.

all sin. I will give you rest from fear, as I become your good shepherd to guard and protect you. I will give you rest from loneliness, as I bring you into the family of God as co-heirs with me of an eternal kingdom. Come, says Jesus, receive me, and in receiving me, receive all this rest. However, Jesus doesn't just leave it there. He presses the invitation home. He doesn't stipulate any extraordinary conditions; He doesn't insist on any prior worthiness. He simply says, 'Take My yoke upon you and learn from Me' (Matt. 11:29). In other words, become my disciple. In so coming to me Jesus says, you will find me no hard teacher. I am kind and gentle, and I will deliver the rest I invite you to: 'I am gentle and lowly in heart, and you will find rest for your souls. For My yoke is easy and My burden is light' (Matt. 11:29-30). This is the gospel invitation, to come to a gracious, loving Saviour, and find rest in Him.

The Gospel as an Entreaty

The gospel is an invitation. But it is more than that. It is a pleading, and entreaty. We see this clearly in 2 Corinthians 5:20, where the apostle Paul says, 'Now then, we are ambassadors for Christ, as though God were pleading through us: we implore *you* on Christ's behalf, be reconciled to God.' Paul presents the gospel to the Corinthian church, 'pleading' and 'imploring'. The invitations of the gospel are soaked with every ounce of emotional energy, as a father pleading with his son not to ruin his life, or a mother imploring her daughter to turn from a destructive path. This is the nature of the gospel invitation.

We see the same picture in Romans 10:21. Paul here is again discussing Israel's rejection of the gospel. Israel has the gospel of a Saviour to come preached to them: 'How beautiful are the feet of those who preach the gospel of peace, Who bring glad tidings of good things!' (Rom. 10:15 – Paul is citing Isa.

52:7 and Nahum 1:15). Yet Israel continually turned away from the gospel, leading to the cry of Isaiah 53:1, 'Lord, who has believed our report?' (cited in Rom. 10:16). This rejection of Israel was not the rejection of a dispassionate gospel invitation. Israel's rejection was in the face of God pleading with gospel-despising Israel: 'All day long I have stretched out My hands to a disobedient and contrary people' (Rom. 10:21 – citing Isa. 65:2).

Accordingly, the posture of the gospel invitation is of a father with outstretched arms, waiting for and begging his wayward children to come home. The gospel is an entreaty, it is to be shared with beseeching, with tears, with open arms. As Charles Hodges says, 'The stretching forth the hands is the gesture of invitation, and even supplication. God has extended wide his arms, and urged men frequently and long to return to his love; and it is only those who refuse, that he finally rejects.'[4]

The Gospel as a Sale

The gospel offer is also described in the Bible as a selling. The classic passage which does this is Isaiah 55, and particularly verses 1-3. There the gospel is compared to a great food market, but all that is on offer is available at no cost, 'Ho! Everyone who thirsts, Come to the waters; And you who have no money, Come, buy and eat. Yes, come, buy wine and milk Without money and without price.' What is obvious in any selling process is that you want to close the sale, you want the goods or service to be purchased. That is the same here in Isaiah.

Isaiah pictures the gospel under the image of food and water. The gospel gives water to the spiritually thirsty, water that springs up into everlasting life (John 4:13-14). That water

---

4. Charles Hodge, *The Epistle to the Romans* (Repr.; London: Banner of Truth, 1972), 350.

is Jesus: 'On the last day, that great *day* of the feast, Jesus stood and cried out, saying, "If anyone thirsts, let him come to Me and drink"' (John 7:37). The gospel gives bread to the hungry, and that bread again is Jesus: 'Jesus said to them, "I am the bread of life. He who comes to Me shall never hunger"' (John 6:35). In Isaiah 55, Jesus is put up for sale. But at what cost or price? What has to be done to buy Jesus? Well, Isaiah tells us: absolutely nothing. This glorious salvation, this glorious Saviour, is available to 'you who have no money' (Isa. 55:1). There are no requirements to be met in order to be able to accept the invitation: 'Yes, come, buy wine and milk Without money and without price' (Isa. 55:1). In other words, take the gospel, take Jesus Christ as the bread of life and the fountain of living water springing up into eternal life, receive Him freely, with no worthiness required on your part. All that is necessary as a 'price' is simply to come empty-handed to faith in Jesus.

But, despite this wonderful offer, many do not take up the invitation to have Jesus. As a result, Isaiah goes on to plead: 'Why do you spend money for *what is* not bread, And your wages for *what* does not satisfy?' (Isa. 55:2). Compared to what He is offering (and for free!) what the people are wasting their time and money on is worthless. They are giving their lives to what ultimately leaves them empty. He calls them to realise this, and then he continues: 'Listen carefully to Me, and eat *what is* good, And let your soul delight itself in abundance' (Isa. 55:2). Consider, use your reason, discern the difference between the worthless things that consume your life's energies and the good news of the gospel. See the abundance of spiritual fare that is available for free in Jesus Christ.

To show His earnestness God repeats His invitation: 'Incline your ear, and come to Me' (Isa. 55:3). There must be no doubt that the invitation should be accepted, and so God pleads, listen, come to me. He presses on to induce acceptance by promising great blessings to those who do accept the invitation. Come to Jesus and find life (Isa. 55:3) and in finding life receive the blessing of an everlasting covenant, 'Hear, and your soul shall live; I will make an everlasting covenant with you – The sure mercies of David' (Isa. 55:3). Come, accept the offered sale of Jesus and in accepting find security, a covenant bond with the living God that can never be broken.

David had been promised an everlasting Kingdom: 'And your house and your kingdom shall be established forever before you. Your throne shall be established forever' (2 Sam. 7:16). What Isaiah is saying, is that if we accept God's salvation, freely available, then we enter into this unbreakable kingdom. We ultimately come under the reign of the greater than David, King Jesus. In Him we are secure for all eternity in unbroken kingdom fellowship with the triune God, and His people. Who would refuse such a gift, freely offered for sale, for as has been said, here we have 'the best wares at the lowest rates'?[5]

The Gospel as Standing and Knocking

Another image used in picturing the gospel is of someone standing outside a house, knocking at a door and desiring entry. We are given this picture in Revelation 3:20: 'Behold, I stand at the door and knock. If anyone hears My voice and opens the door, I will come in to him and dine with him, and he with Me.' This is a familiar picture, and often used in evangelism, but it is sometimes questioned whether this verse speaks of the gospel offer. After all, is this verse not in a letter to a church, and so, isn't it calling believers into restored fellowship with Christ, rather than presenting a gospel call? The two ideas aren't mutually exclusive. To believers in the Church, no doubt this is calling for restored fellowship, but for unbelievers

---

5. Durham, *Unsearchable Riches*, 136-160.

in the Church surely this is a gospel call to saving faith. The evidence regarding the church in Laodicea, to whom this letter is addressed, is that they were largely unregenerate.

The church in Laodicea is described variously as 'neither cold nor hot' (Rev. 3:15), about to be 'vomit[ed] … out of My mouth' (Rev. 3:16), and 'wretched, miserable, poor, blind, and naked' (Rev. 3:17). They are urged to 'buy from Me gold refined in the fire, that you may be rich; and white garments, that you may be clothed, *that* the shame of your nakedness may not be revealed; and anoint your eyes with eye salve, that you may see' (Rev. 3:18). Surely this tells us that because Laodicea lacked the 'unsearchable riches of Christ' in their hearts, they needed to buy gold. They were without the righteousness of Christ to clothe them, leading to the necessity for the 'white garment' of Christ's righteousness. Spiritual blindness characterised them, and they needed gospel salve for their eyes to give spiritual sight. Unregenerate churches like this can exist, where the gospel light has all but been extinguished and unbelievers are in the vast majority.

To these unsaved people, Jesus comes and says that He stands knocking, desiring admittance into their hearts and offering them the gospel feast of His wonderful saving fellowship. We are not to be ashamed of images like this. Christ in the gospel, through the word and common operations of the Spirit, knocks on the hearts of all. This does not render Him impotent. As J. I. Packer has noted, Revelation 3:20 does not show 'the impotence of His grace apart from man's cooperation… but rather the grace of His omnipotence in freely offering Himself to needy souls.'[6] This same Jesus standing knocking is the one who opens and no one can shut, and who shuts and no one can open (Rev. 3:7). Jesus is always sovereign, but in grace here He

---

6. J. I. Packer, 'The Puritan View of Preaching the Gospel,' in *How Shall they Hear?* (Puritan & Reformed Studies Conference, 1959), 18.

simply knocks and gives inducement for sinners to open the doors of their hearts. Yes, the saving grace of God is needed to enable the knocking to be answered, and the closed door of the heart to be opened, but that does not remove the genuineness of the knocking, nor the truth of the inducement that 'I will come in to him and dine with him, and he with Me' (Rev. 3:20).

The gospel offer, then, is rightly pictured as a standing and knocking. Indeed, James Durham paraphrased this verse as saying, 'I come in my gospel to woo, and, if any will consent to take me on the terms on which I offer myself, I will be theirs.'[7]

The Gospel as a Command

The gospel offer is additionally a command. The invitation to come to Christ is an invitation that must be accepted. When Christ knocks, we must open the doors of our hearts. Paul shows us this when he is before the Areopagus in Athens. Paul addressed the 'very religious' Athenians (Acts 17:22) outlining their innate sense of a need to worship even in ignorance (Acts 17:23), declaring to them the true Creator God (Acts 17:24-25), bringing home their relation to the true God (Acts 17:26-28) and showing them, in the light of this, the folly of their idolatry (Acts 17:29).

Having laid that foundation Paul moved on to declare the gospel to them. He concludes his 'sermon' saying, 'Truly, these times of ignorance God overlooked, but now commands all men everywhere to repent, because He has appointed a day on which He will judge the world in righteousness by the Man whom He has ordained. He has given assurance of this to all by raising Him from the dead' (Acts 17:30-31). These Athenians are commanded to repent, they are commanded to turn from their idols to trust in Jesus Christ. The gospel isn't something

---

7.   Durham, *Unsearchable Riches*, 46.

that can be trifled with. There is a day of judgment coming, when the resurrected Jesus will say to each individual either 'Come, you blessed of My Father, inherit the kingdom prepared for you from the foundation of the world' (Matt. 25:34) or 'Depart from Me, you cursed, into the everlasting fire prepared for the devil and his angels' (Matt. 25:41). So, it is a matter of great importance to believe in Jesus Christ now. This is a command to avoid danger. It is a command for our own safety. This is how Paul preached the gospel before the Areopagus.

This gospel command is also urgent. There is a need to comply now because on the day of judgment it will be too late: 'Seek the Lord while He may be found, Call upon Him while He is near' (Isa. 55:6). At the present time there is the command to repent with the promise of acceptance: 'Turn at my rebuke; Surely I will pour out my spirit on you; I will make my words known to you' (Prov. 1:23). But if the command to turn, to repent is rejected now, then a sad and desperate day will soon come. God speaks of a day when, 'Because you disdained all my counsel, And would have none of my rebuke, I also will laugh at your calamity; I will mock when your terror comes' (Prov. 1:25-26). On that day, there will be a desire to comply with the command to repent, but it will be too late. If we reject the urgent command now this judgment of God will rest on us: 'Then they will call on me, but I will not answer; They will seek me diligently, but they will not find me. Because they hated knowledge And did not choose the fear of the Lord, They would have none of my counsel *And* despised my every rebuke. Therefore they shall eat the fruit of their own way, And be filled to the full with their own fancies' (Prov. 1:28-31). Now is the day of salvation, now is the time to listen to God's urgent command.

The apostle John also shows us the gospel offer as a command. He says: 'And this is His commandment: that we should believe on the name of His Son Jesus Christ' (1 John 3:23). The gospel focuses on Jesus Christ. His person and work are the good news, so that 'If we confess our sins, He is faithful and just to forgive us *our* sins and to cleanse us from all unrighteousness' (1 John 1:9). It is Jesus as 'the propitiation for our sins, and not for ours only but also for the whole world' who is the gospel (1 John 2:2). Our relation to this Jesus should not be a matter of debate or indifference. Whether we should have anything to do with Him is not an open question. The gospel comes and *commands* us to believe in the name of Jesus, that name that was given to Him because He would save His people from their sins (Matt. 1:21). The gospel commands us to receive the Saviour of the world as our Saviour.

The Gospel as a Warning

The gospel is an invitation. At the same time the gospel also contains a note of warning. However, even these warnings, when truly understood, can be thought of as good news. To be warned of danger is a helpful thing. The warning at the beach 'Danger: strong tides' is good news if it saves lives and prevents drownings. Just like the beach sign the gospel carries with it its own warnings. A classic example is found in Hebrews 2:3: 'How shall we escape if we neglect so great a salvation, which at the first began to be spoken by the Lord, and was confirmed to us by those who heard *Him*'? The salvation preached in the Bible is indeed 'great'. It is the message of eternal life to those who are dead in sins (Col. 2:13). It is the proclamation of liberty to those who are captives to sin (Luke 4:18). It is the heralding of adoption into the family of God for those who are by nature children of wrath (Eph. 2:3-4). Its message is simple: believe on the Lord Jesus and all this is yours (Acts 16:31). But, and here is the warning, if we neglect this salvation, there is no other means of being reconciled to God. There is no other escape from the 'wrath to come' (Matt. 3:7). If the salvation we are invited to in Jesus Christ is spurned, all that remains is the doom: 'But the … unbelieving … shall have their part in the lake which burns with fire and brimstone, which is the second death' (Rev. 21:8). To reject Jesus is to bring yourself into this state of condemnation, for, 'he who does not believe is condemned already, because he has not believed in the name of the only begotten Son of God' (John 3:18).

This is unspeakably solemn. Yet the note of warning always accompanies the faithful preaching of the gospel. Our Saviour Himself consistently taught 'unless you repent you will all likewise perish' (Luke 13:3). He was very clear on what perishing meant. To perish is to be 'cast … into the outer darkness' where 'there will be weeping and gnashing of teeth' (Matt. 25:30). To perish is to be consigned to 'this place of torment' (Luke 16:28) where 'Their worm does not die And the fire is not quenched' (Mark 9:44, 45, 48). In a measure faithful preaching of the good news can be discerned by how often the warning note sounds. It is integral to gospel preaching.

The Gospel as a Promise

However, to end a discussion of what the gospel offer means with the note of warning would not be right. Fundamentally the gospel is good news. And so, this chapter closes with the gospel as a promise. Scripture contains two kinds of promises – unconditional and conditional. Unconditional promises are those such as the foundational covenant promise, 'I will be your God, and you shall be my people' (for example, Gen. 17:7; Exod. 6:7; Ezek. 34:24, 36:28; Jer. 7:23, 30:22, 31:33). Or the great promise of Romans 8:28, 'And we know that all things work together for good to those who love God, to those who are the called according to *His* purpose.' These promises are unilateral commitments from God; they are unbreakable words from the covenant-keeping God.

Other promises, by contrast, are conditional. They depend on something being done. The preaching of the gospel contains a glorious, though conditional promise. Just consider perhaps the most famous 'gospel' verse, John 3:16: 'For God so loved the world that He gave His only begotten Son, that whoever believes in Him should not perish but have everlasting life.' Here is a precious conditional promise. Anyone who believes in Jesus is delivered from everlasting perishing, and instead will know eternal life.

The same promise is seen in dealing with the spiritual case of individuals. In Acts 16 we find Paul in Philippi. Soon opposition arises to the gospel, and Paul and his companion Silas are imprisoned (Acts 16:24). At midnight while Paul and Silas were praying and praising God in the prison there was an earthquake (Acts 16:25-26). But this was no ordinary earthquake, as the consequence was 'immediately all the doors were opened and everyone's chains were loosed' (Acts 16:26). Waking and seeing the prison doors opened, the prison keeper thought all his prisoners had escaped and he moved to kill himself, but was prevented by Paul crying out, 'Do yourself no harm, for we are all here' (Acts 16:27-28). The jailor was so moved by this that he cried out, 'Sirs, what must I do to be saved?' (Acts 16:30). To this distressed cry he received the promise, 'Believe on the Lord Jesus Christ, and you will be saved, you and your household' (Acts 16:31). The gospel comes and promises to this man on the verge of ending his life, that if he believes in Jesus salvation will be his. Immediately he embraced this promise and so, 'he rejoiced, having believed in God' (Acts 16:34).

Embedded, then, in the gospel is this wonderful conditional promise of salvation. This promise is to be freely proclaimed to every gospel hearer. This is the point Paul makes in Romans 10. He states that the distinction between Jew and Gentile has now been abolished, for 'the same Lord over all is rich to all who call upon Him' (Rom. 10:12). The proof of this barrier between Israel and the rest of the world having been removed is that, 'whoever calls on the name of the Lord shall be saved' (Rom 10:13). The gospel promise (Acts 16:31) brings everyone who hears the gospel into this position: armed with a promise, encouraged to believe in Jesus, knowing certainly that in so doing they will be saved. This is the gospel offer.

4

WHO GIVES AND RECEIVES THE GOSPEL OFFER?

God offers ... all good, and freely ... O how good is God to offer
spiritual good to sinners! O how patient is God even to sinners,
who neglect the offers of his Grace!
Obadiah Sedgwick (1600-1658)[1]

There is a wonderful richness in the many ways scripture describes the gospel offer, ranging from invitation and entreaty through to command and warning. But who does all these things? Who offers the gospel? Is it simply the preacher or evangelist, or is it God Himself who offers the gospel? And to whom is the gospel offer directed? Is it a subset of hearers, the spiritually thirsty, the spiritually burdened, or is the offer for all hearers of the gospel? Consideration will now be given to these questions.

---

1. Obadiah Sedgwick, *The Fountain Opened: and the Water of Life Flowing forth to thirsty sinners. Wherein is set out, Christ's earnest and gracious invitation of poor sinners to come unto the waters* (London: T. R. and E. M. for Adoniram Byfield, 1657), 2.

Who Gives the Gospel Offer?

It is clear that the gospel offer is given through human agency. Preachers audibly proclaim the gospel in their sermons. In evangelism the man or woman evangelising offers Christ to those they are engaging with. But behind this is a glorious truth: the real offerer of the gospel is God. Fundamentally, it is God who invites, who pleads, who sells, who knocks, who commands, who warns and who promises.

We see God Himself repeatedly offering the good news of the gospel in the Old Testament. From the earliest times God is active in dealings with sinful humanity. After the wreckage of the fall, and the abounding of sin on the earth, we read, 'And the Lord said, "My Spirit shall not strive with man forever, for he *is* indeed flesh"' (Gen. 6:3). In the days before the flood destroyed the world, God was at work through His Spirit calling the world to Himself. While Noah was 'a preacher of righteousness' (2 Pet. 2:5), ultimately it was God's Spirit calling men and women to obedience.

When we move into the prophetic era in the Old Testament, from Moses onwards, we find that the prophets did not deliver their own message, but spoke God's message. So, when the prophets called Israel to embrace the gospel, in reality the call was from God Himself. The New Testament tells us that 'prophecy never came by the will of man, but holy men of God spoke *as they were* moved by the Holy Spirit' (2 Pet. 1:21). The ideas the prophets communicated were not dreamt up by them; they were the very words given them by God. Moses, and all prophets including the great prophet Jesus, prophesied under this rule: 'I will ... put My words in His mouth, and He shall speak to them all that I command Him' (Deut. 18:18). Therefore, at the end of his life when Moses preaches, 'I have set before you life and death, blessing and cursing; therefore choose life, that both you and your descendants may live'

64

(Deut. 30:19), this isn't his word only. It is fundamentally the Lord, not Moses, who is calling on Israel to choose the life they repeatedly spurned and rejected.

2 Chronicles 36:15-16 helps us see clearly that the gospel invitations of the prophets were also God's personal invitations. We are told there:

> the Lord God of their fathers sent *warnings* to them by His messengers, rising up early and sending *them,* because He had compassion on His people and on His dwelling place. But they mocked the messengers of God, despised His words, and scoffed at His prophets.

So, when the prophets spoke to Israel they did so as God's messengers, and if they were rejected it was the very Word of God that the people 'despised.' Every call to repentance, to receive mercy, to have sins forgiven was a call from the living God. That is why we have the complaint of God in Psalm 81:13, 'Oh, that My people would listen to Me, That Israel would walk in My ways!' It was God who was calling them.

Isaiah and Jeremiah also show us that the prophets were not speaking their own words, but relaying God's gospel offers. In Isaiah. 1:18 we have God pleading, 'Come now, and let us reason together, Says the Lord, Though your sins are like scarlet, They shall be as white as snow; Though they are red like crimson, They shall be as wool.' In Jeremiah 2:9 (KJV) we hear of God's continual pleading with His people: 'Wherefore I will yet plead with you, saith the LORD, and with your children's children will I plead.' In Jeremiah 7:13 God protests, 'I spoke to you, rising up early and speaking, but you did not hear, and I called you, but you did not answer.' Many more examples could be given but the point is incontrovertible. In the Old Testament, God Himself offered the good news of forgiveness from sins. When His prophets spoke, He spoke.

Moving into the New Testament, we see that just as God offered the gospel in the Old Testament, His Son, Jesus Christ Himself, offers the gospel in the New Testament. Jesus' public ministry recorded in Mark begins: 'Now after John was put in prison, Jesus came to Galilee, preaching the gospel of the kingdom of God, and saying, "The time is fulfilled, and the kingdom of God is at hand. Repent, and believe in the gospel"' (Mark 1:15). Jesus Himself says He came 'to call … sinners to repentance' (Mark 2:17). Examples of Jesus doing just this are commonplace in the Gospels. In John 4:14 as Jesus is conversing with the Samaritan woman, He says to her, 'If you knew the gift of God, and who it is who says to you, Give Me a drink, you would have asked Him, and He would have given you living water.' In John 7:37-38, Jesus issues the same invitation to receive living water from Him, not to one person but to a large crowd: 'If anyone thirsts, let him come to Me and drink. He who believes in Me, as the Scripture has said, out of his heart will flow rivers of living water.' In Matthew 11:28 there is the invitation to all people, whatever sins and burdens they carry, 'Come to Me, all *you* who labour and are heavy laden, and I will give you rest.'

In giving these (and many other) invitations Jesus is not simply reflecting His humanity, but He is speaking as the God-man. His invitations are the invitations of God the Son, speaking in harmony with the Father and Spirit. We can say of Jesus' gospel invitations, 'My teaching is not my own. It comes from the one who sent me' (John 7:16, NIV) and 'the word which you hear is not Mine but the Father's who sent Me' (John 14:24). When we read in the Gospels of Jesus issuing invitations to sinners to come to Him we can say, 'He who has Me has seen the Father' (John 14:9). When we see Jesus tenderly inviting sinners to Himself, we can say we have before us 'the image of the invisible God' (Col. 1:15). When

Jesus weeps over the rejection of His gospel offers (Luke 19:41), there as much as ever He remains, 'the brightness of *His* glory and the express image of His person' (Heb. 1:3). Yes, there is humanity in Jesus' tears, but that is simply the sinless human display of the Divine compassion evidenced in His universal gospel offer. We are never to imagine Jesus as more loving and merciful than the Father or the Spirit. Jesus does not earn for us the love and compassion of the Father. Rather, it is because of the Father's love for lost sinners that God the Son came into the world (John 3:16). Jesus' gospel compassion and His invitations reveal to us the great triune God of scripture.

After the death, resurrection and ascension of the Lord Jesus, God still continues to offer the gospel. He now does this through His written Word, and gospel preachers. The key verse which shows us that the gospel invitation is God's invitation is 2 Corinthians 5:20. Paul has just explained the great fact of the gospel, namely 'that God was in Christ reconciling the world to Himself, not imputing their trespasses to them' (2 Cor. 5:19). He has told us that this message needs to be preached, what Paul calls 'the word of reconciliation' (2 Cor. 5:19).

How is this gospel word of reconciliation through the death of Christ to be preached, and on what basis? Paul gives us a startling answer: 'Now then, we are ambassadors for Christ, as though God were pleading through us: we implore *you* on Christ's behalf, be reconciled to God' (2 Cor. 5:20). Preaching the 'word of reconciliation' involves imploring, appealing, urging and begging hearers to accept the Lord Jesus Christ and the reconciliation with God accomplished by Him. But what is more, this imploring is not just the preacher's. Paul says that the preacher is simply an 'ambassador for Christ' and so it is 'as though God were pleading through us'. The preacher's pleading is God's pleading because the preacher, like the Old Testament prophet, has no words of his own. They are ambassadors, they are to have no message except the one their King gives them. In the words of John Murray, 'it is as ambassadors on behalf of Christ, and as of God beseeching through them, that the preachers of the evangel pray men to be reconciled to God.'[2] And so, gospel invitations, gospel pleadings in preaching do not belong to the preacher only: they are God's Word to lost sinners.

This is reinforced by the parable we have considered before in Matthew 22:1-14 (and Luke 14:16-24). The King sends invitations for the great wedding feast. His servant's role is not to create their own invitations, but simply to deliver the invitation of the King. We read: 'At the time of the banquet he sent his servant to tell those who had been invited, Come, for everything is now ready' (Luke 14:17, NIV). This image shows clearly that the gospel invitation is God's. The role of God's servants is merely to deliver it!

The final gospel invitation in all of scripture, in Rev. 22:17, puts beyond any doubt (if any were left) that it is God who offers the gospel. We read, 'And the Spirit and the bride say, Come! And let him who hears say, Come! And let him who thirsts come. Whoever desires, let him take the water of life freely.' The repetition of 'Come' emphasises the urgent, pressing nature of the invitation. It is a gracious and infinitely bountiful invitation as shown by the word 'freely'. In essence, it is the same gospel invitation issued in Isaiah 55:1 and John 7:37-38. But who gives the invitation to come? First of all, God Himself, for here God the Spirit says, come! The Church as the bride of Christ echoes this invitation to come, as do individual believers within the Church, those who themselves have heard the invitation. The gospel invitation normally goes through us and is delivered by human agency, but fundamentally it is God's invitation to come and take the water of life freely. As John

---

2. Murray, *Collected Writings*, 1:85.

Murray has said, 'It is Christ in all the glory of his person and in all the perfection of his finished work **whom God offers** in the gospel.'[3]

To Whom is the Gospel Offer Directed?

If God gives the gospel invitation, who does He invite? Who does He offer His Son Jesus Christ to as Saviour? Is it to just His chosen elect people? Is it only to those who have earned the right to receive the invitation? Or does God invite all to come to Him, and be saved?

In one sense these might seem questions that don't need to be asked. It is evident that as God 'commands all men everywhere to repent' (Acts 17:30) the gospel is for all. It is hard to conceive of a statement more universal than 'all … everywhere'. The angel announcing the birth of the Saviour said, 'I bring you good tidings of great joy which shall be to all people' (Luke 2:10). But there have been many who have found it hard to believe the good news of the gospel is for them, especially in the context of God's sovereignty. If God has chosen who to save, how can I know the gospel is for me? It is important to counter that line of thinking by being clear on the scriptural testimony that the gospel invitation is for all.

We can see this universal nature of the gospel in that it is for the whole world. Even in the Old Testament, with its focus on the nation of Israel, there were calls for the world to come to God for salvation: 'Look to Me, and be saved, All you ends of the earth! For I *am* God, and *there is* no other' (Isa. 45:22). When wisdom called for people to listen to her, her voice was not to one nation but to humanity: 'To you, O men, I call, And my voice *is* to the sons of men' (Prov. 8:4). And this universal call to salvation is heightened in the New Testament, for the

---

3. Murray, *Collected Writings*, 4:132.

'great commission' charges the Church to take the message of the risen and ascended Jesus to every nation. The task which Jesus committed to His disciples was, 'that repentance and remission of sins should be preached in His name to all nations' (Luke 24:47, c.f. Matt. 28:18-20, Mark 16:15). No part of the world is excluded, no individual in the world is excluded. Every nation, and every individual within every nation, is to have the offer of forgiveness in Jesus Christ made to them. As Calvin says, 'He invites the whole world to the hope of salvation'.[4]

Since the gospel is to go out to all, everywhere, it is framed in the universal form of 'whoever' to ensure no one feels excluded. The most famous example is John 3:16: 'For God so loved the world that He gave His only begotten Son, that whoever believes in Him should not perish but have everlasting life.' There is no fence put up around believing in Jesus. There are no qualifications, ethnic or spiritual, but simply the universal whoever. The salvation that there is in Jesus Christ is for whoever will believe and embrace it. Calvin helpfully comments on the word whosoever, 'he has used a general universal term, both to invite indiscriminately all to share in life and to cut off every excuse from unbelievers.'[5]

This was exactly the message that the apostles preached in Acts. In Peter's sermon on the day of Pentecost he preached, citing Joel 2:32, that 'whoever calls on the name of the Lord shall be saved' (Acts 2:21). Later when Peter is himself wrestling with the universal implications of the gospel being for Jew and Gentile he returns to the same truth. Because 'whoever believes in Him will receive remission of sins,' Peter understands that salvation is for all (Acts 10:43). Paul picks up on the same point

---

4.   Calvin, *Calvin's Commentaries*, 8:425.
5.   John Calvin, *Calvin's New Testament Commentaries* (Eds. David W. Torrance and Thomas F. Torrance; Trans. by various; 12 vols.; Carlisle: Paternoster, 1995), 4:74.

in Romans 10 to show that the gospel is for all. He reasons, 'there is no distinction between Jew and Greek, for the same Lord over all is rich to all who call upon Him. For whoever calls on the name of the Lord shall be saved' (Rom 10:12-13). He removes any suggestion that the gospel is only for special categories of people with the word 'whoever', indeed 'no sorts of men are excluded from the remedy but those that exclude themselves by their impenitency and unbelief.'[6]

It is instructive that the last gospel invitation in the Bible contains this unmistakably universal note. God, as we have seen, gives the gospel offer in Revelation 22:17 in this form: 'Whoever desires, let him take the water of life freely.' None are excluded. Anyone who wants may come and be saved. And to return again to the apostolic preaching in Acts, this is exactly what we see time and again: mixed gatherings of those who will accept the gospel, and those who will reject it, receiving the gospel invitation that 'whoever desires' might receive Jesus Christ. After calling his hearers to repentance and assuring them that if they do they will receive remission of sins, Peter says this promise of forgiveness is 'to you and to your children, and to all who are afar off, as many as the Lord our God will call' (Acts 2:39). All whom God calls in the gospel offer receive this conditional promise of forgiveness, none excluded. Paul, preaching in Antioch, tells a mixed crowd in the synagogue, not all of whom would believe, 'Let it be known to you, brethren, that through this Man is preached to you the forgiveness of sins' (Acts 13:38). When Paul is in Athens his gospel preaching is not restricted to specific hearers but he offered Christ 'in the marketplace daily' to 'those who happened to be there' (Acts 17:17). Even in the last picture we have of Paul in Acts, being under house arrest in Rome, does not prevent him offering

---

6. Thomas Manton, *The Works of Thomas Manton*, (22 vols.; repr.; Edinburgh: Banner of Truth, 2020), 2:348.

the gospel. 'Many' we are told came to his lodgings, and Paul sought to 'persuade them concerning Jesus from both the Law of Moses and the Prophets, from morning till evening' (Acts 28:23). As usual when the gospel was preached, 'some were persuaded ... and some disbelieved' (Acts 28:24). But this made no difference to who the gospel was offered to; it was offered to every hearer. And this is a good summary of Paul's universal practice: invite all, try to persuade all, regardless of the truth that some will believe and some will not. This biblical focus on the task rather than results is an important corrective for our results-focused age.

The rest of the Bible is equally clear that the gospel is not restricted to any specific group. Isaiah 1:18 is a wonderful gospel offer: 'Come now, and let us reason together, Says the Lord, Though your sins are like scarlet, They shall be as white as snow; Though they are red like crimson, They shall be as wool.' But the context is clear, that those to whom the offer is made are those utterly unconcerned about their spiritual state. They are wallowing in their sins. Even animals know their master, God complains, '*but* Israel does not know, My people do not consider' her maker and her God (Isa. 1:3). Israel are 'A people laden with iniquity, A brood of evildoers' who 'have forsaken the Lord' and turned their back on Him (Isa. 1:4). Israel has sunk so low, that God addresses her as Sodom and Gomorrah: 'Hear the word of the Lord, You rulers of Sodom; Give ear to the law of our God, You people of Gomorrah' (Isa. 1:10). Yet to this people, God offers cleansing and forgiveness. Nor were this and many other offers made by God through Isaiah accepted. The complaint 'Who has believed our report? And to whom has the arm of the Lord been revealed?' (Isa. 53:1) surrounds all Isaiah's gospel proclamations. Israel had no spiritual qualifications, but she still received the gospel invitation.

Paul reflects on this in Romans 10. In Romans 10:21 (citing Isa. 65:2) he refers to God saying, 'All day long I have stretched out My hands To a disobedient and contrary people.' Israel were not longing for the invitation, quite the opposite. It had no attraction for them. That is why we can be certain that the invitation is not restricted – it is given to those who have no interest in it. God stretches out His hands in the gospel offer to many hearers who will simply reject it, while all the time saving some, even who themselves had no interest when God first invited them to Himself. If the invitation did not go to those who spurn it, Jesus could hardly have wept over its refusal (Luke 19:41, 42).

The gospel offer then goes to all, no matter how deeply ensnared in sin and uninterested they may appear. In Ezekiel God says that He has no pleasure in the death of the wicked, but would rather that the wicked turn from their ways and live (Ezek. 18:23, 32; 33:11). That is why the gospel offer is not restricted. God has no pleasure in the death of any; therefore all are called to repent and believe. The gospel comes to all and says, 'This *is* a faithful saying and worthy of all acceptance, that Christ Jesus came into the world to save sinners, of whom I am chief' (1 Tim. 1:15). The gospel is truly worthy of acceptance by all, and it is offered to all.

This understanding of a gospel for all leads to preaching like that of James Durham:

> We make this offer to all of you, to you who are atheists, to you who are graceless, to you who are ignorant, to you who are hypocrites, to you who are lazy and lukewarm, to the civil and to the profane. We pray, we beseech, we beg you all to come to the wedding … we do most really offer Him [Christ]

to you all, and it shall be your own fault if you lack Him and go without Him.[7]

But What About the Restrictions?

If this is so clear then why have there been many who have worried that the gospel isn't for them? One cause of this misplaced anxiety is the biblical passages which appear to restrict the gospel offer, either by limiting its geographical scope or inviting a sub-group of hearers to embrace the good news. Paul, for instance, is told not to preach the gospel to the Roman province of Asia and Bithynia (Acts 16:6-7). Yes, but Paul is only one person, and that temporary restriction was there because Paul had gospel work to do in Macedonia (Acts 16:10). Perhaps requiring more careful thought are passages which seem to address the gospel invitation to those who are 'thirsty' or who are 'heavy laden'. Examples here are Isaiah 55:1-3 and Matthew 11:28.

Looking first at Isaiah 55, at a glance it may appear that the gospel is restricted to the 'thirsty'. Isaiah 55:1 reads, 'Ho! Everyone who thirsts, Come to the waters; And you who have no money, Come, buy and eat.' It seems only the 'thirsty' are invited. But who does Isaiah mean by the thirsty? In Isaiah, a lack of water or being in thirst, indicates the judgment of God against sin. We see this in the very first chapter where God threatens judgment: 'For you shall be like an oak whose leaf withers, and like a garden without water' (Isa. 1:30, ESV). Later in Isaiah we are told, 'For behold, the Lord God of hosts is taking away from Jerusalem and from Judah support and supply, all support of bread, and all support of water' (Isa. 3:1, ESV). This tying together of judgment against sin and drought

---

7. Durham, *Unsearchable Riches*, 60.

is not unique to Isaiah. Think of the life of Elijah. Elijah prayed 'fervently that it might not rain, and for three years and six months it did not rain' (James 5:17, ESV). And he prayed for this drought as a *judgment* upon the sin of Israel. Or think of the most pre-eminent example of undergoing the judgment of God, the Lord Jesus Christ on the cross. And what did Christ cry, on the cross while laying down His life for His sheep, and experiencing the wrath of God against sin? 'I thirst' (John 19:28).

So, when Isaiah says 'come everyone who thirsts' he is not restricting the invitation, but rather saying 'Come sinners, come sinners under the judgment of God.' And that is every individual. All are under the judgment of God, all are 'thirsty' for the removal of that judgment however much they suppress that knowledge in unrighteousness (Rom. 1:18). Everyone is thirsty, because by nature everyone has 'forsaken me, the fountain of living waters, and hewed out cisterns for themselves, broken cisterns that can hold no water' (Jer. 2:13, ESV).

We see further that Isaiah is not restricting his invitation only to those qualified in some way by having a spiritual thirst because he invites those with 'no money' (Isa. 55:1). No one earns access to this invitation by 'thirsting' as some qualifying mark. That would be to bring 'money'. Rather the invitation is free. It is to spiritual bankrupts. For example, if we have the idea that we must make ourselves better before we can embrace the gospel by living so long without a certain sin, Isaiah 55 says no, as that would be to bring money, your own works to earn access to Jesus. Or, if we think we have to have sorrowed over sin for so long, or reached a certain depth of conviction over our sins before we can accept the good news, again that would be to try and earn something for something that must be accepted freely. So, we could understand Isaiah like this: 'He who has no money, come' means 'You who have nothing, you who have wasted all that God has given you in sin, you who have nothing to commend yourselves to God, come.'

Preaching on this verse James Durham also argued against any limitation on the gospel offer. He said that the gospel offer was not restricted to those who could say that they had experienced deep conviction of sin as a 'qualification' to accept the invitation, 'Nay, in some way it excludes these, as offering to bring money and some price, which would quite spoil the market of free grace; nay yet, I say further, if it were possible that a soul could come without sense of sin, grace would embrace it.'[8]

Matthew 11:28 presents us with a similar invitation to Isaiah 11. There Jesus says, 'Come to Me, all *you* who labour and are heavy laden, and I will give you rest.' It has also been argued in the past that Jesus only invites those who feel the burden of their sins. Now it is true that only those who are sick go to the doctor, and only those who are aware they are sinners will go to the Saviour (Matt. 9:12). The gospel is for sinners not the righteous (Matt. 9:13), though of course all are sinners (Rom. 3:23). But Jesus here isn't requiring us to qualify ourselves by having a great sense of sin, and being burdened by it, and labouring under it for a long time. Rather Jesus knows that all in the world 'spend money for *what is* not bread, And your wages for *what* does not satisfy' (Isa. 55:2). He knows that at the end, the experience of all 'under the sun' is, 'For what has man for all his labour, and for the striving of his heart with which he has toiled under the sun? For all his days *are* sorrowful, and his work burdensome; even in the night his heart takes no rest. This also is vanity' (Eccles. 2:22-23). Jesus knows all are burdened. So His invitation to find rest in Him

---

8. Durham, *Unsearchable Riches*, 156-7.

is not restrictive: it speaks to all who hear it, for 'sinners, while out of Christ, are engaged in a wearisome labour.'[9]

Conclusion

It is one of the wonders of this life, that God Himself, offers rest in Jesus to every sinner who hears His gospel, inviting all to receive salvation in Christ. As Thomas Boston has said, 'If you could make these invitations of your own framing, could you make them more comprehensive?'[10] But these all-encompassing invitations are not simply to be wondered at, they are to be embraced, and received. We now turn to encouragements to do just that.

---

9. Boston, *Works*, 9:175.
10. Boston, *Works*, 3:268.

5

ENCOURAGEMENT TO ACCEPT THE OFFER

If any man shall not be taken with the sweet invitation of God,
nor with the humble and loving request of God, made to him
to be reconciled, he shall find he hath to do with the sovereign
authority of the highest Majesty; for 'this is his commandment,
that we believe in him,' saith he.
The Sum of Saving Knowledge (1650)[1]

The gospel invitation is for all. But what are we to do when we receive the gospel offer? Is there to be any doubt that it should be received? Strangely there has been perplexity on this simple and straightforward point. Some have placed the doctrine of election as a barrier, saying that they can't accept the invitation until they know that they are among the few chosen rather than just among the many called (Matt. 22:14). Others have said that they have no strength at all to accept the invitation because, as we are dead in sins, we don't have the ability to accept. We should just sit and wait until God works life in us. Others raise questions around who Jesus died for. If He laid down His life for the sheep, don't I need to know I am one of

---

1. 'The Sum of Saving Knowledge' in *Westminster Confession of Faith &c.* (Glasgow: Free Presbyterian Publications, 1994), 336.

them before I believe? Given these concerns, why can we say that all should accept the gospel invitation? What should give any and all the confidence to come to Jesus?

We Are Invited

As we have seen, the gospel offer is an invitation. By definition an invitation carries with it the right to be accepted. You do not worry about whether you have the right to accept an invitation to a wedding when it is in your hands. The invitation itself gives you that right. And it is the same with the gospel. No one who hears the gospel should question whether they have the right to receive Jesus Christ as Saviour. Whatever sins, whatever past rejection of the gospel, even the 'chief of sinners' can accept the invitation (1 Tim. 1:15).

We can see this clearly by discussing one of the 'gospel invitation' texts. The Gospel of John itself is fundamentally an evangelistic tract. It is written with the burden 'that you may believe that Jesus is the Christ, the Son of God, and that believing you may have life in His name' (John 20:31). That evangelistic thrust underlies the whole gospel, but it is seldom clearer than in John 7:37-38, where Jesus as *the* great evangelist invites sinners to come to Him for salvation: 'On the last day, that great day of the feast, Jesus stood and cried out, saying, If anyone thirsts, let him come to Me and drink. He who believes in Me, as the Scripture has said, out of his heart will flow rivers of living water.'

The obvious feature of this invitation to highlight is that it is to those in need. Those invited are 'thirsty'. Clearly this is a common image. The youngest child knows what it is to be thirsty, after playing a hard game of football, or running round with friends in the sun.

But what specifically does Jesus mean here? What need is He highlighting? What spiritual realities are represented by this image of 'thirst'? As we saw in the previous chapter, this image is of those at a distance from God, and often under His judgment. So, Jesus is saying: 'If anyone is at a distance from God ... come to me.'

There is another example in John's gospel of Jesus inviting someone who was far from God to come to Him for the water of life. In John 4 Jesus meets the woman of Samaria. Here was a woman who was surely far from the fellowship of God, indeed she was clearly under the displeasure and judgment of God. She had previously had five husbands, and the one she was now living with was not even her husband. When she met Christ she had no thirst for righteousness, but she had a thirst for something and was trying to satisfy that thirst in an immoral lifestyle. But her thirst would not be quenched. Husbands one to five had failed to do this, and so had her current partner. As Augustine said, 'You have made us for yourself, and our heart is restless until it finds its rest in you.'[2] To this thirsty woman Jesus said, 'Whoever drinks of the water that I shall give him will never thirst. But the water that I shall give him will become in him a fountain of water springing up into everlasting life' (John 4:14).

So, it is to sinners in great need, like the woman of Samaria, that Jesus later says, 'If anyone thirsts, let him come to Me and drink.' And it is to all those in need: 'If *anyone* thirsts, let him come to Me and drink.' No one is excluded from Jesus' invitation here; all are encompassed by it. This is a universal invitation to meet a universal need. Everyone needs these waters, for as Calvin commenting on this verse notes, 'we are

---

2. Saint Augustine, *Confessions: A new translation by Henry Chadwick* (trans. Henry Chadwick; Oxford: Oxford University Press, 2008), 3.

---

indeed all poor and empty and destitute of all blessings.'[3] Jesus invites all to Himself, because all are thirsty.

The universality of the invitation is also emphasised by the context in which Jesus delivered it. The invitation was delivered at the 'feast of tabernacles' (John 7:2). This in itself tells us that the invitation was issued at a time where there would have been large crowds of people. Again, the invitation was issued on 'the great day of the feast' (John 7:37) where numbers would be at their peak. Also, in giving the invitation Jesus 'cried out' (John 7:37). He issued the invitation in a way to ensure the greatest number of people would hear. All these pointers show Jesus wished His invitation to come to Him to be as universal as possible.

The invitation is also full of patience. In John 7:12 a number of those at the feast had rejected Jesus: 'There was much complaining among the people concerning Him'. We see that Jesus is accused of having a demon (John 7:20). We see in that He is accused of not being the Christ: 'We know where this man is from; but when the Christ comes, no one knows where he is from' (John 7:27). We see that He is under threat of being taken into custody (John 7:30). Yet Jesus persists in teaching the people and inviting them to Himself for salvation.

There is also an encouragement to accept the invitation: 'He who believes in Me, as the Scripture has said, out of his heart will flow rivers of living water' (John 7:38). For those who embrace the invitation, there is the promise of the indwelling of the Holy Spirit. This is how John explains it: 'But this He spoke concerning the Spirit, whom those believing in Him would receive' (John 7:39). What a blessing it is to have the Holy Spirit. The Spirit is the one who assures us that we are Christians (Rom. 8:16). It is the Spirit who gives us the ability to know God as Father (Rom. 8:15). It is the Spirit who works

---

3.   Calvin, *Calvin's New Testament Commentaries*, 4:197.

Christian graces in us (Gal. 5:22-23). It is the 'Holy Spirit of promise, who is the guarantee of our inheritance until the redemption of the purchased possession, to the praise of His glory.' (Eph. 1:13-14). It is the Spirit who helps us evangelise others (John 16:7-8). What a promise this is to encourage the acceptance of the invitation. To be shown that believing in Jesus leads to the blessings of a Spirit filled life of assurance of sins forgiven, a sure status as children of God, and a guarantee of glory to come for all eternity, is to be given a heaven-sent incentive to respond to the gospel.

With this before us, who would doubt they should accept the gospel invitation?

God Pleads With Us

We can also be sure all who hear the gospel have a right to accept it because God pleads with us to embrace the good news. It is not just that all are invited to accept the gospel, it is that God beseeches all who hear the gospel to receive it. It is as if having an invitation, someone phones up to urge, to plead, that the invitation be accepted.

We see this many times in the Old Testament, where God pleads with His people to turn to Him. One example that is frequently referred to is in Ezekiel 18. There Israel, in exile in Babylon, are expressing their dissatisfaction with God. They complained that 'The fathers have eaten sour grapes, And the children's teeth are set on edge' (Ezek. 18:1). That is, the previous generations sinned, and this generation of Israelites were suffering unjustly because of that. The continued exile in Babylon was in their eyes an act of God's caprice, rather than an act of justice. Against this false accusation God patiently explains how He deals with individuals (Ezek. 18:4-18). Fundamentally, God says, any repentant individuals will be viewed in the light of their repentance, and not in the light of their own or a previous generation's sins (Ezek. 18:14-17). The Lord explains why this is so, saying, 'Do I have any pleasure at all that the wicked should die? says the Lord God, *and* not that he should turn from his ways and live?' (Ezek. 18:23). The character of God's very being is against the hypothesis that Israel was propounding. For Him to delight in the destruction of a subsequent repentant generation (or individual) is inconceivable: it gives Him no pleasure. Rather than delight in the death of the wicked, God delights in the repentance of the wicked. Calvin helpfully deduces from this verse that 'God desires nothing more earnestly than that those who were perishing and rushing to destruction should return into the way of safety.'[4]

In light of this Israel was to cease their false accusations against God (Ezek. 18:24-29). Ezekiel's message is 'Repent, and turn from all your transgressions, so that iniquity will not be your ruin' (Ezek. 18:30). God goes on and pleads with His recalcitrant people: 'For why should you die, O house of Israel? For I have no pleasure in the death of one who dies, says the Lord God. Therefore turn and live!' (Ezek. 18:31-32). God says, there is no reason for you to die in your sins. There is no reason for you to stand afar off, questioning me. As I have said, consider my character. Know that I truly have no desire that you die in your sins. Because of who I am, listen to me. Consider, turn to me and know that in doing so you will live; eternal life will be yours. Here is God pleading, reasoning, with His people who had hearts of bitterness towards Him. What greater inducement could they receive than that to come to God for salvation?

But the charges against God's fairness continued, and are largely repeated in Ezekiel 33:12-20. Still Israel complained,

---

4. Calvin, *Calvin's Commentaries*, 12:246.

'If our transgressions and our sins *lie* upon us, and we pine away in them, how can we then live?' (Ezek. 33:10). God responded as He had done earlier. He again reminded them of the nature of His character, and on that basis pleaded with them to cease their accusations and to turn to Him. Ezekiel was commissioned, 'Say to them: *As* I live, says the Lord God, I have no pleasure in the death of the wicked, but that the wicked turn from his way and live. Turn, turn from your evil ways! For why should you die, O house of Israel?' (Ezek. 33:11). The pleading has reached staggering levels. So insistent is God that the accusation against Him is unjust, that He takes an oath by Himself, 'As I live'. On the basis of that oath He explains His character again: He has no pleasure in the death of the wicked, but rather does have pleasure in their salvation. Having sworn this is true, God pleads on this basis, 'Turn, turn from your evil ways! For why should you die, O house of Israel?' Again, and again, God pleads showing His people they have every right to come to Him.

This pleading continues in the New Testament. 2 Corinthians 5:20 is a verse we have considered before. But it is central to the encouragement to accept Jesus Christ. It reads: 'Now then, we are ambassadors for Christ, as though God were pleading through us: we implore *you* on Christ's behalf, be reconciled to God.' Here the New Testament mode of gospel presentation is set before us: imploring hearers to be reconciled to God, to receive Jesus Christ in His saving work (2 Cor. 5:21). Preachers are to be 'fishers of men' (Matt. 4:19). As fishermen seek to catch fish, so God's ambassadors seek by all means to persuade sinners that only through faith in Jesus can the breach with God be overcome: 'I have become all things to all *men,* that I might by all means save some' (1 Cor. 9:22).

This earnest, affectionate, pleading is on behalf of the Lord Jesus. It is God's pleading. So, here is God pleading, yet again, for reconciliation with alienated sinners. Here is God seeking for friendship with those who are His enemies, begging them to turn away from enmity with Him, and be at peace through His Son. How can any doubt they should accept the gospel message, when this is the image of how it should be presented to us? As James Durham has said, 'To have a gracious offer from God, and to fear at it, as if He were not in earnest, is very unbecoming the gospel. Whenever He pipes, it becomes us well to dance, and to believe and credit Him when He speaks fair and comfortably.'[5]

God Commands Us to Accept

So, all who hear the gospel have a right to accept Jesus as Saviour, because they are invited and because God pleads with them. But there is a further heightened reason all should embrace the gospel. More than all having good reasons to embrace God's invitation, they have a fundamental duty to receive Jesus, because God commands them to. If any doubt they should receive Jesus, if invitations and pleading are not enough, these doubts are silenced by the command of God: 'And this is His commandment: that we should believe on the name of His Son Jesus Christ' (1 John 3:23).

The phrase 'duty faith' has been employed by critics of the teaching that every person is commanded to believe. This term puts the teaching in a very negative light, suggesting that, instead of true faith which is a product of divine grace, faith is being turned into an outward response and a human accomplishment. But there is no doubting the clear testimony of scripture that all have a *duty* to believe because it is a commandment of God. We are used to thinking there is a requirement to do as God tells us, to obey the Ten Commandments and in doing so to love

---

5.   Durham, *Unsearchable Riches*, 96.

God, and to love our neighbour as ourselves (Matt. 22:37-39). But accepting Jesus as Saviour is no less a command of God.

John 6:28-29 corroborates the truth we saw previously in 1 John 3:23. The context here is that Jesus has just fed the five thousand (John 6:1-14). Jesus, not being willing to submit to false ideas about Him establishing an earthly kingdom (John 6:15), departed from the crowd and (after walking on the sea to re-join His disciples!) ended up in Capernaum. When the crowd eventually find him there, Jesus has hard words for them. He says to them that they have sought Him not because they understood who He was, but because they 'ate of the loaves and were filled' (John 6:26). Recognising this was their position Jesus exhorts them: 'Do not labour for the food which perishes, but for the food which endures to everlasting life, which the Son of Man will give you, because God the Father has set His seal on Him' (John 6:27). Perplexed, the crowd ask Jesus, 'What must we do to do the works God requires?' (John 6:28, NIV). In other words, what is it God commands us to do then? To which Jesus replies, 'This is the work of God, that you believe in Him whom He sent' (John 6:29). This is all that God commands, not great works of righteousness, not great effort. The work that God wants, the obedience God wants, is to believe in Jesus. This is His command, and it shows all need to believe in Jesus Christ.

But what if it is said, the command is unfair? It is asking those who have no ability to believe to do what is impossible for them. If people are dead in trespasses and sins (Eph. 2:1), what is the use in commanding them to believe? Well, it is true that none will believe without God's saving work. But that does not mean the gospel command has nothing to do with us. It is clear, we can understand it, and the command to believe is fair because no one is compelled to disobey it. Those who refuse the command, do so because they want to refuse.

Jesus' words in John 5:40 are instructive. He diagnoses the root cause of unbelief not in inability, but in unwillingness: 'But you are not willing to come to Me that you may have life.' Or again in Matthew 23:37, 'How often I wanted to gather your children together, as a hen gathers her chicks under *her* wings, but you were not willing!' God has the right to command men as He pleases. Nothing compels any to disobey, except their own stubborn unwillingness. God does not tempt any into sin (James 1:13), and this includes the sin of unbelief. So, the rejection of the gospel cannot be excused on account of God's sovereignty and our inability, for 'each one is tempted when he is drawn away by his own desires and enticed' (James 1:14).

God Warns Us Not to Refuse

Another encouragement to believe is God's warning against unbelief. When God gives warnings of judgment to come, He does so not because He delights in judgment, but in order that repentance might come and prevent the judgment. We see this clearly in the book of Jonah. Jonah is given a commission: 'Arise, go to Nineveh, that great city, and cry out against it; for their wickedness has come up before Me' (Jonah 1:2). In the well-known sequel he refuses his task, runs away and it is only when swallowed by a great fish while fleeing that he accepts the foolishness of his disobedience. But why did Jonah flee? It was not because he was concerned about the Ninevites. Quite the opposite. He was very content with their destruction. The issue was that he knew God's announcement of judgment was a call to Nineveh to repent, and that God would accept their repentance. That is exactly what happened. Nineveh repented, 'and God relented from the disaster that He had said He would bring upon them, and He did not do it' (Jonah 3:10). Jonah threw this back in God's face: 'But it displeased

Jonah exceedingly, and he became angry … I fled previously to Tarshish; for I know that You *are* a gracious and merciful God, slow to anger and abundant in lovingkindness, One who relents from doing harm' (Jonah 4:1-2). Jonah wasn't happy, but he had God's character exactly right. God is gracious and loving, therefore His warnings of judgment are a call to repent and turn to Him.

The Bible does not shy away from the consequences of unbelief. It is clear that belief leads to eternal life, and unbelief to eternal death (Deut. 30:19). It is clear that there is a hell for unbelievers, a place of 'wailing and gnashing of teeth' (Matt. 8:12, 13:42, 13:50, 22:13, 24:51, 25:30; Luke 13:28), a place of 'outer darkness' (Matt. 8:12, 22:13, 25:30; Jude 1:13), of eternal fire (Isa. 66:24; Matt. 18:8, 25:41; Mark 9:43, 48; Rev. 19:20, 20:10, 20:14-15, 21:8), of torment in the conscience (Mark. 9:44, 48), of eternal destruction (2 Thess. 1:9). It is clear that unbelief leads to this condemnation (John 3:18-19; Mark 16:16). It is clear that there is no escape for those who neglect the great salvation there is in Jesus Christ (Heb. 2:2).

This clarity is there, not to delight in judgment, but to persuade sinners to flee from the wrath to come, to cry to God for mercy, and to embrace the mercy offered to the world in Jesus Christ. We are encouraged to accept Jesus, by God in love warning us of the consequence of not accepting the Saviour of the world. This was Paul's reasoning: 'Knowing, therefore, the terror of the Lord, we persuade men' (2 Cor. 5:11).

An All-Sufficient Saviour for a Universal Need

Commands, warnings, pleadings and invitations all tells us that we can receive Jesus Christ without doubt or question. But one further inducement to believe, is that Jesus is the all sufficient Saviour that all need.

We saw in chapter 1 that 'all have sinned and fall short of the glory of God' (Rom. 3:23). All are under the curse of death (Rom. 6:23) and judgment (Gal. 3:10). This can be seen clearly in the life of Saul of Tarsus, the man who would become the apostle Paul. Reflecting back on his early life after his conversion he styles himself the 'chief of sinners' (1 Tim. 1:15). Why does he describe himself in that way? Did he commit some of the foulest crimes which cause public outrage? Was he shunned by his fellows as a reprobate? Was he notorious?

Not at all. He was a highly respected Pharisee taught by the leading Rabbi Gamaliel. Outwardly, he was as 'good' as it was possible to be. The Pharisees stood for rigorous obedience to the Mosaic law. But despite claiming that he was blameless concerning the righteousness which was in the law (Philippians 3:6), his heart was full of sin, leading Saul of Tarsus to be a bitter persecutor of the Christian Church. When the Lord dramatically appeared to him on the road to Damascus, Saul was going there 'breathing threats and murder against the disciples of the Lord' (Acts 9:1, ESV). He describes himself as a 'blasphemer' and an 'insolent opponent' (1 Tim. 1:13, ESV). But, despite his flagrant persecution of the Church, that is not what Jesus puts His finger on. Instead the Lord says: 'I am Jesus whom you are persecuting' (Acts 9:5). His greatest sin, his spiritual crime, was his fanatical hatred of the Lord, revealed in the fury of his attack on the believers. This man, regarded as holy and good, was a great sinner, indeed the great sinner. Truly there is none righteous, no not one (Rom. 3:10).

How could there be salvation for so great a sinner as Saul? Because of the sufficiency of the blood of Jesus to cleanse from all sin (1 John 1:7). Because there is not one sin so great that the atoning work of Jesus cannot propitiate the wrath of God against it, even a sinner like Saul could be saved. Yes, in love, Jesus died for His Church, His bride (Eph. 5:25). But the death of Jesus is sufficient to blot out any and all sin, and save any and every sinner who seeks shelter from wrath under the cover of His atonement. It is because Jesus' death is of infinite merit that He can promise never to cast out any who come to Him (John 6:37), that He can save to the uttermost all who come to God through Him (Heb. 7:25). Jesus will save, through His death and resurrection, every kind of sinner from 'every nation, from all tribes and peoples and languages' (Rev. 7:9, ESV). We can never doubt the sufficiency of Christ's atonement to save us. Again, John Murray is helpful: 'The gospel comes to him as an unsaved sinner and its demand is that he commit himself to Christ … What intrudes to justify this entrustment is the all sufficiency and suitability of the Saviour and the Saviour's own word in the free overture of his grace.'[6]

So, there is mercy, apostle-making mercy, for Saul the arch-rejecter. Christ's merit is sufficient to save even the greatest of sinners. The conclusion from this must be that the greatest sin, and the only sin which disqualifies anyone from salvation, is continued rejection of Christ. Only a lifelong rejection of the invitation of free grace and forgiveness condemns us in the face of gospel mercy.

It is this truth that Paul the apostle, now freed from a religious zeal for establishing his own righteousness and an intense bitterness against the Saviour, sought to spread throughout the world. In Antioch of Pisidia he announces to the Jews, 'Let it be known, therefore, to you, brothers, that through this man forgiveness of sins is proclaimed to you' (Acts 13:38 ESV). He urges the pagans at Lystra to turn from idols to the living God. (Acts 14:15). In Romans 10:13, like Peter on the Day of Pentecost, he quotes Joel 2:32: 'For whosoever shall call upon

---

6.   Murray, *Collected Writings*, 1:84.

the name of the Lord shall be saved' (KJV). He urges Timothy in 2 Timothy 4:5 to 'do the work of an evangelist'. Paul's firm commitment to the sovereignty of God (e.g. Rom. 9) was no barrier to his pressing every sinner to embrace the all sufficient gospel.

So, it is simply the perversity of sin and the blasphemy of unbelief to argue that the gospel cannot save us and that the gospel invitation is not for us. It denies the power of the blood of Christ. It denies that the Saviour came to seek and to save that which was lost. Christ's ministry in the gospels builds up a picture of a loving, committed, seeking God who delights to find and save and receive. The old saying of John 'Rabbi' Duncan is graphic and true: 'Men evangelised cannot go to hell but over … God's great mercies. They must wade to it through the blood of Christ.'[7]

It is equally perverse to use the truth of election to deny the truth of Christ's acceptance of anyone and everyone who comes to Him for salvation. Only coming to Christ can give assurance of salvation and therefore of being among God's people. Election is God's business; responding to God's gracious invitation is ours. Every questioning of our right or fitness is unbelief. Our only fitness is our sinnership. The gospel is for sinners. Everyone is a sinner. Therefore, the gospel is for everyone. It is for hardened sinners, it is for fearful sinners, it is for self-righteous sinners – sinners of every stripe. The invitation is there. The invitation is pressing. The invitation demands a response.

---

7. John Duncan, *Just a Talker: The Sayings of Dr John Duncan* (Edinburgh: Banner of Truth, 1997), 221.

6

GOD'S WILL AND THE GOSPEL

As many as are called by the gospel, are unfeignedly called; for God hath most earnestly and truly declared in his Word what will be acceptable to him, namely, that all who are called should comply with the invitation. He, moreover, seriously promises eternal life and rest to as many as shall come to him, and believe on him.
Canons of Dort, Article 3/4:8 (1619)[1]

All receive the gospel offer, and all are encouraged to accept it. But does God really want my salvation? Does God want me to believe in Jesus and be saved? After making an important theological distinction, the answer we will see is, yes and yes!

Understanding the Will of God

One of the great Christian prayers is: 'Your will be done On earth as *it is* in heaven' (Matt. 6:10). The desire expressed in this prayer is that the sinless situation in heaven, where nothing takes place that is contrary to God's good commands, is replicated on earth. We are praying for our actions to become aligned to God's commands (His will for us), that is, to love Him with all

---

1. Philip Schaff, *The Creeds of Christendom* (3 vols.; repr., Grand Rapids: Baker, 1993), 3:589.

our heart, soul, strength and mind and love our neighbour as ourselves (Luke 10:27). However, it is evident that God's will in the sense of His commands, His revealed will for us, is often not done. Life in this world is not like heaven. So we need to pray God's will would be done.

Two references to God's will in 1 Thessalonians reinforce for us that God's will is often not done. Paul says: 'This is the will of God, your sanctification: that you should abstain from sexual immorality' (1 Thess. 4:3). God's will is that, as part of their sanctification, Christians do not partake in sexual activity outside of marriage. However, it is a sad reality of life that God's people do fail in this area. So, God's will here is what He wants His people to do, not what He has infallibly decreed they will do. Similarly, in 1 Thessalonians 5:18 we are exhorted: 'In everything give thanks; for this is the will of God in Christ Jesus for you.' God's will is that Christians are thankful people. But, again, we know that not all Christians are like this, and certainly not all the time! Again, God's will is evidently not done in many cases.

But God's will not being carried out in practice creates a problem. Have we not seen when considering the sovereignty of God that 'Whatever the Lord pleases He does, In heaven and in earth, In the seas and in all deep places' (Ps. 135:6)? Have we not seen that God 'works all things according to the counsel of His will' (Eph. 1:11)? Absolutely. God reigns sovereign over all things. Not one of His purposes can fail. It is an immovable and unshakable truth that 'The counsel of the Lord stands forever, The plans of His heart to all generations.' (Ps. 33:11). Whatever we do, there can be no doubt when God says:

> My counsel shall stand,
> And I will do all My pleasure (Isa. 46:10).

We need somehow to relate these two different ways of speaking of God's will where in one sense God's will is not done but in another sense God's will is always done. Do we do this by concluding that God has two wills? No, for while scripture holds out these realities to us, it also insists that God's will is one. God's being is a great unity: 'Hear, O Israel: The Lord our God, the Lord *is* one!' (Deut. 6:4).

Given this, there needs to be a recognition that we are finite creatures and cannot fully fathom the greatness of God's being. Our limitations mean the one will of God may *appear* manifold from our perspective. The position can be summarised as follows: God's will is one but from our limited perspective we cannot see and grasp the full range and harmony of that will, so we have to speak of that one will in varied ways. That is simply part and parcel of a recognition that God is beyond our comprehension (Isa. 55:8-9). As John Murray has said, 'it is not the mark of intelligence to claim a ready resolution of the apparent contradiction with which [this] confronts us.'[2] We have to accept that any wrestling with a subject like the will of God will leave us exclaiming, 'Oh, the depth of the riches both of the wisdom and knowledge of God! How unsearchable *are* His judgments and His ways past finding out!' (Rom. 11:33).

So, while holding that God's will must be one, we have to make a distinction to make sense of the breadth of scriptural revelation. To help us make this distinction, consider the death of the Lord Jesus Christ. In one sense it was obviously the will of God that Jesus die as the once for all sacrifice for sins. He died as a result of 'the determined purpose and foreknowledge of God' (Acts 2:23). We are told that 'it was the Lord's will to crush him and cause him to suffer' (Isa. 53:10, NIV). Jesus' death was not a happenstance. He was 'the Lamb slain from the foundation of the world' (Rev. 13:8).

---

2. Murray, *Collected Writings*, 4:202.

But laid beside this are the equally clear teachings that the death of Jesus was forbidden by God. The death of Jesus was a sinful act, i.e. contrary to the will of God expressed in His law: 'Jesus of Nazareth ... you have taken by lawless hands, have crucified, and put to death' (Acts 2:22-23). It was an act inspired by the very devil himself: 'Then Satan entered Judas, surnamed Iscariot, who was numbered among the twelve' (Luke 22:3). Pilate, who oversaw the trial of Jesus, was warned not to allow His condemnation: 'Have nothing to do with that just Man, for I have suffered many things today in a dream because of Him' (Matt. 27:19). So, in these, and other ways, the death of Jesus was contrary to the will of God.

To bring these two disparate 'wills' together we need to distinguish between what is called God's will of decree and God's commanding will. The former is what God has decreed as to what will happen (Christ will die), the latter is God's directive will (the innocent should not be put to death).[3] Both reveal God's one will but in different ways. The decretive will is largely secret. It is God working out His purposes in ways we cannot see or understand. It is a will that is always done. The commanding will, by contrast, is revealed to us. It tells us what things God delights in, and which things He abhors, considered as they are in themselves. As William Cunningham has written, 'the law is an expression of the divine will, and indicates that, in some sense, God wishes, as He commands and enjoins, that all His rational creatures should ever walk in

---

3. In what follows I broadly equate God's directive or commanding will with His revealed will for us. However, there is a broader way of speaking of God's revealed will where it has a more obvious overlap with God's secret will. For instance, we could say in one sense God's revealed will is that His Son should die (Isa. 53:8-9), in that God has revealed it must happen to bring about salvation. Generally though I will use 'revealed' as an equivalent to 'command', and so in this sense God's revealed will is that no one should kill His Son (Exod. 20:13).

the ways of holiness; and that all men doing so, should be for ever blessed.[4]

God's decretive will mysteriously and wondrously ordains things which are contrary to what God delights in for greater good (as in the death of Christ). But we must always hold fast to the truth that God's revealed and directive will tells us what He delights in, it reveals those things which He as a merciful and holy God takes pleasure in. Because God's will is one, therefore His secret will is always in harmony with His revealed will. As His revealed will is good, so also His secret will is good. As Calvin has said, 'this is exactly our belief, that His will is one and undivided: but because our minds cannot plumb the profound depths of his secret election to suit our infirmity, the will of God is set before us as double.'[5] Faith in God means we must give our attention to this revealed will, and not tie ourselves in knots over the will of decree, for 'The secret *things belong* to the Lord our God, but those *things which are* revealed *belong* to us and to our children forever, that *we* may do all the words of this law' (Deut. 29:29).

God's Revealed Will is His Delight

Let us focus now on how we are to understand the revealed will of God, His 'commanding will', His precepts and His delights. What does God's revealed will *reveal* about God? The simple answer to this is that it tells us what is pleasing to God, what He wants us to do. We are told this in Romans 12:2 where Paul exhorts, 'Do not be conformed to this world, but be transformed by the renewing of your mind, that you may prove what *is* that good and acceptable and perfect will

4. William Cunningham, *Historical Theology* (2 vols.; repr.; Edmonton: Still Water Revival Books, 1991), 2:452.

5. John Calvin, *Calvin's New Testament Commentaries*, 3:69.

of God.' Here Paul tells the Roman believers to 'renew their minds,' which we can take as seeking the Spirit's transforming of our thinking and motivation through the teaching of scripture. That transformation would lead them to the place where 'by testing you may discern what is the will of God' (ESV). This isn't and can't be the will of God's decree, for that is and remains His 'secret' (Deut. 29:29). What we have here is a better discerning of the *revealed* will of God as we get to know His Word better. And that revealed will is described as 'good and acceptable and perfect'. God's revealed will discloses what is good, and therefore what is acceptable or 'pleasing' (NIV) to Him as a revelation of His perfect nature.

When God gives a command, it is a legitimate deduction that it is pleasing to Him. As Calvin says, 'God gives no insincere precepts but seriously reveals what he wills and commands.'[6] When God calls us to love Him and to love our neighbour as ourselves (Mark 12:30-31) it is clear that these are pleasing things that God wants us to do. To do these things is to 'do His will' which 'is well pleasing in His sight' (Heb. 13:21).[7] Conversely to fail to do what God asks is to displease Him. We are told, 'For You *are* not a God who takes pleasure in wickedness' (Ps. 5:4) Similarly, when Israel disregarded God's 'calls' to them they 'chose *that* in which I do not delight' (Isa. 66:4).

We have seen that God commands that the gospel offer is accepted. God 'commands all men everywhere to repent'

6.   John Calvin, *The Secret Providence of God* (Trans. P. Helm; Wheaton, IL: Crossway, 2010), 100.

7.   There are occasions where God commands His people to do things which He ordinarily has no pleasure in. For example, the command to Hosea to marry 'a wife of harlotry' (Hos. 1:2). Yet, while contrary to God's revealed will (Exod. 20:14) Hosea was bound to believe, by virtue of the specific command he received, that what he was called to do was pleasing to God. In the case of Hosea, the greater purpose was to picture God's grace to a wayward people.

(Acts. 17:30). Taking this command seriously, it must reveal that God desires, God wants people to embrace the gospel offer. This is pleasing to Him. The rejection of the gospel offer is not what He wants. It is displeasing and contrary to His delights. But we do not simply have to rely on implications. Both the Old and New Testaments make it abundantly clear that God wants His gospel embraced by all who hear it, none excepted.

The Revealed Will and the Gospel in the Old Testament

One truth that is frequently presented in the Old Testament is that God *wants* His people to embrace the salvation He offers in the gospel. This is embedded in the earliest books of the Bible, the Pentateuch. In Deuteronomy Moses recounts to Israel God's dealings with them in their wilderness journeys from Egypt to the borders of the Promised Land. Specifically, in Deuteronomy 5 he tells how God gave the Ten Commandments at Mount Sinai. The people responded by saying that they would 'hear and do' all God desired (Deut. 5:27). But God knew the heart of the people and so He exclaimed to Moses in response, 'Oh, that they had such a heart in them that they would fear Me and always keep all My commandments, that it might be well with them and with their children forever!' (Deut. 5:29). What we have here is a clear declaration from God that He wishes Israel would truly and really embrace Him as their redeemer, as 'the Lord your God who brought you out of the land of Egypt, out of the house of bondage' (Deut. 5:6). Now the Lord had not, according to His sovereign will of decree, determined that Israel would wholly follow Him. But that is no barrier to God expressing that He delights in Israel trusting in Him as they should. God here desires, as something pleasing to Him, that Israel would be saved. It is truly a sad matter, a grieving thing for Israel to reject, as they so often did, their Saviour. As Calvin preached on this verse, 'we have [a] matter of record that he is desirous to be at one with us, and to do the duty of a father … God wisheth that we should do the things he commandeth us, to the intent that it might go well with us.'[8]

This rejection is contrary to God's desire and pleasure because it is contrary to His revealed intention in giving Israel the gospel. In Deuteronomy 30, after God has recounted the blessings and curses of the Law, He said, 'The word *is* very near you, in your mouth and in your heart, that you may do it' (Deut. 30:14). God set His redemption before His people, for the principal purpose that they embrace it. That is why Israel's rejection of the gospel causes God to say: 'Oh, that they were wise, *that* they understood this, *That* they would consider their latter end!' (Deut. 32:29). There is a longing expressed here that Israel would receive the life offered to them. God would be pleased with that, and wished that it was so. But it was not to be.

The same idea as we have in Deuteronomy is expressed in Psalm 81. This Psalm, like Deuteronomy, reflects on Israel's deliverance from Egypt and how that called them to truly receive the gospel: 'I *am* the Lord your God, Who brought you out of the land of Egypt; Open your mouth wide, and I will fill it' (Ps. 81:10). However, the Psalm recognises the sad history of Israel, and their rejection of their God: 'But My people would not heed My voice, And Israel would *have* none of Me. So I gave them over to their own stubborn heart, To walk in their own counsels' (Ps. 81:11-12). Again, though, this is not as God desired things to be. Rather God cries out: 'Oh, that My people would listen to Me, That Israel would walk in My ways!' (Ps. 81:13). The image here is one of lament. Like a grieved parent who desires obedient and loving children, and who does every

---

8.   John Calvin, *Sermons on Deuteronomy* (Trans. Arthur Golding; repr.; Edinburgh: Banner of Truth, 1987), 260-1.

good he possibly can for them, God groans and expresses His wish for His people to follow Him that He might shower blessing on them (Ps. 81:14-16). There can be no doubt this expresses God's pleasure in Israel's salvation, and His desire that they would turn to Him, even though ultimately many of them did not. As Calvin says, 'There is the justest [well founded] ground for saying that he wills the salvation of those to whom that language [i.e. of Ps. 81:13] is addressed.'[9]

Isaiah similarly teaches on many occasions God's desire for Israel's salvation in His revealed will. We see this in the first chapter of Isaiah. The chapter opens with God bewailing the behaviour of His children: 'I have nourished and brought up children, And they have rebelled against Me; The ox knows its owner And the donkey its master's crib; But Israel does not know, My people do not consider' (Isa. 1:2-3). Israel's treatment of God is incomprehensible. He has been good to them; He has treated them so well. But they do not even show Him the same favour that an animal shows its owner. Yet, notwithstanding this, notwithstanding the depth of Israel's sin, God still calls to them: 'Come now, and let us reason together, Says the Lord, Though your sins are like scarlet, They shall be as white as snow; Though they are red like crimson, They shall be as wool' (Isa. 1:18). Why would God come again to them with the gospel? A people so underserving? A people whose sins call out so loudly for judgment? Simply because God's gospel offer is genuine, it is sincere, it reflects God's pleasure that all sinners come to Him and have the guilt of their sins washed away.

God goes to great lengths to show the reality of His desire for the salvation of rebellious, resistant sinners. In Isaiah 5 God takes up a controversy with Israel. He portrays them under the image of a vineyard, with Him as the vinedresser. As the vinedresser, God has done all things well for His vineyard. It is

---

9.   Calvin, *Calvin's Commentaries*, 5:324-5.

on a 'very fruitful hill' (Isa. 5:1). It has been dug and cleared from stones; the vine stock used to plant the vineyard is 'the choicest' (Isa. 5:2). Everything is there for this vineyard to produce 'good grapes'; indeed a tower and winepress have been prepared in the vineyard in expectation of this (Isa. 5:2). However, despite all God did for Israel, 'it brought forth wild grapes'. Only bad fruit was produced (Isa. 5:2). This leads God to exclaim: 'What more could have been done to My vineyard That I have not done in it? Why then, when I expected *it* to bring forth *good* grapes, Did it bring forth wild grapes?' (Isa. 5:4). Everything had been done for this vineyard. Nothing was lacking. Similarly, spiritually for Israel nothing was lacking. God, again and again, sent His prophets to draw Israel to embrace the gospel (2 Chron. 36:15). But despite all this, despite everything God did to demonstrate His desire for Israel to embrace Him, He was left to ask: 'Yet I had planted you a noble vine, a seed of highest quality. How then have you turned before Me Into the degenerate plant of an alien vine?' (Jer. 2:21). Israel's degeneration, and their subsequent judgment, was in no way due to a lack of desire in God to show them mercy in the gospel.

We see this again later in Isaiah. In Isaiah 48 God, through His prophet, is ministering to His people who have been exiled to Babylon for their sins. This judgment on them for being a rebellious people was under the control of the one who is utterly sovereign: 'I *am* He, I *am* the First, I *am* also the Last. Indeed My hand has laid the foundation of the earth, And My right hand has stretched out the heavens; *When* I call to them, They stand up together' (Isa. 48:12-13). Consequently, when the time was right God would lead His people on a new exodus from Babylon, back to the Promised Land (Isa. 48:21). But what is clear from this passage is that God's pleasure was not in the exile. This was an act necessitated by Israel rejecting the will and pleasure of God. God explains to Israel who He is, and what He has done for them in Isaiah 48:17: 'Thus says the Lord, your Redeemer, The Holy One of Israel: I *am* the Lord your God, Who teaches you to profit, Who leads you by the way you should go.' God is the Saviour, His gospel is good for His people, His commands show them what is pleasing to Him. Yet Israel have rejected this, and judgment came on them. But God wished it was not so: 'Oh, that you had heeded My commandments! Then your peace would have been like a river, And your righteousness like the waves of the sea' (Isa. 48:18). John Murray rightly says that in this verse 'the Lord represents himself ... as earnestly desiring the fulfilment of something which he had not in the exercise of his sovereign will actually decreed to come to pass.'[10] It was not God's pleasure for His people to be sent into exile. Rather His desire was that they embrace Him as Saviour and walk in His ways. This same desire gives rise to the gospel invitations like Isaiah 55:1: 'Ho! Everyone who thirsts, Come to the waters; And you who have no money, Come, buy and eat. Yes, come, buy wine and milk Without money and without price.'

Moving on, Jeremiah, despite (or perhaps because of) being a book largely devoted to God's judgment, shows us the same truth: God desires and takes pleasure in salvation, not judgment. Chapter 2 sets the tone in this regard. God asks: 'What injustice have your fathers found in Me, That they have gone far from Me, Have followed idols, And have become idolaters?' (Jer. 2:5). There was nothing in the history of Israel that God had not done for their good. They were redeemed from the slavery of Egypt, they were kept through the wilderness, they were given the Promised Land (Jer. 2:6-7). But against that background Israel did something no other nation had done: 'Has a nation changed *its* gods, Which *are* not gods? But My people have changed their Glory For *what* does not profit' (Jer.

---

10. Murray, *Collected Writings*, 4:119.

2:11, c.f. Jer. 18:15). Indeed, Israel's whole history could really be summed up as: 'They have forsaken Me, the fountain of living waters, *And* hewn themselves cisterns—broken cisterns that can hold no water' (Jer. 2:13). Consequently, judgment came on Israel, but this was not the Lord's desire. Rather it was the result of Israel's sin: 'Have you not brought this on yourself, In that you have forsaken the Lord your God When He led you in the way?' (Jer. 2:17). From the very outset Israel's rejection of God is a grief and a failure to do God's pleasure. But still the gospel offer is made: 'Return, you backsliding children, *And* I will heal your backslidings' (Jer. 3:22). However, it was to fall on deaf ears.

This rejection of the gospel and God's will brings great grief to Jeremiah himself. He cries out, 'O my soul, my soul! I am pained in my very heart!' (Jer. 4:19). He laments in Jeremiah 8:18, 'I would comfort myself in sorrow; My heart *is* faint in me.' And this is because Jeremiah is 'hurt', 'mourning' and 'astonished' (Jer. 8:21) that 'The harvest is past, The summer is ended, And we are not saved!' (Jer. 8:20). This is not due to any lack in God, for there is a balm in Gilead, and there is a physician there. There is a Saviour ready to help, and so the question is genuine: 'Why then is there no recovery For the health of the daughter of my people?' (Jer. 8:22). Jeremiah's mourning in Israel's rejection of their only hope is also sincere: 'Oh, that my head were waters, And my eyes a fountain of tears, That I might weep day and night For the slain of the daughter of my people!' (Jer. 9:1). The same pattern is seen in Jeremiah 13. There the gospel hope is presented again: 'Hear and give ear: Do not be proud, For the Lord has spoken. Give glory to the Lord your God Before He causes darkness' (Jer. 13:15-16). Jeremiah reveals his grief if it will be rejected again: 'But if you will not hear it, My soul will weep in secret for *your* pride; My eyes will weep bitterly And run down with tears, Because the Lord's flock has been taken captive' (Jer. 13:17).

Now, what do we have in the tears of Jeremiah over the destruction of unrepentant Israel? We have nothing other than a human display of the heart of God. Jeremiah here visibly shows to Israel the compassion of their God who 'sent to you all My servants the prophets, rising early and sending *them,* saying, Oh, do not do this abominable thing that I hate!' (Jer. 44:4). The weeping of Jeremiah reveals the heart of God's call: 'Oh, do not do this abominable thing'.

We see this confirmed in Lamentations 3:32-33. There we are told, 'Though He causes grief, Yet He will show compassion According to the multitude of His mercies. For He does not afflict willingly, Nor grieve the children of men.' There is a beautiful balance to these verses. The sovereignty of God is fully in view. Judgment, grief, is under God's control. But this is mingled with compassion and mercy. And this is because 'he does not afflict from his heart or grieve the children of men' (Lam. 3:33, ESV). There is a reluctance on God's part to bring judgment. It is not His pleasure, His joy, His desire. It is His 'strange work', His 'alien act' (Isa. 28:21, NIV). As Thomas Manton has stated, 'Mercy, like live honey, droppeth of its own accord. He is forced to the other [justice]; it is wrested from him.'[11] God's pleasure is in His revealed will.

Perhaps this is most clear in the classic passages in Ezekiel which deal with God's attitude towards the wicked. These have been considered before and so will be mentioned only briefly here. Ezekiel teaches that God never takes pleasure in the death of any wicked person: 'Do I have any pleasure at all that the wicked should die? says the Lord God, *and* not that he should turn from his ways and live?' (Ezek. 18:23). This truth is the very basis for the gospel offer: 'I have no pleasure in the death

---

11. Manton, *Works,* 21:465.

of one who dies, says the Lord God. Therefore turn and live!' (Ezek. 18:32). It is because of the character of God that there is the appeal 'therefore turn and live'. If we do not understand God's desire in His revealed will for all sinners to turn to Him, we undercut the very basis for the gospel appeal, 'turn and live'.

But on no account do we have liberty to deny God's desire for all the wicked to come to Him and live. Ezekiel returns to this same theme in chapter 33. Israel were complaining that their sins would not be forgiven: 'If our transgressions and our sins *lie* upon us, and we pine away in them, how can we then live?' (Ezek. 33:10). And God comes to them and strengthens what He has previously said with an oath: '*As* I live, says the Lord God, I have no pleasure in the death of the wicked, but that the wicked turn from his way and live. Turn, turn from your evil ways! For why should you die, O house of Israel?' (Ezek. 33:11). We cannot deny God's pleasure in any and all sinners turning to Him without denying the very being of our God. Seeing as He could swear by no greater that this is true, God swore by Himself, by His own eternal superabundant life. He has set His own life as the seal that He desires all sinners to repent and find life. And because of this the compassionate loving call goes forth, 'Turn, turn from your evil ways'. God's gospel offer is not a bare command disconnected from who He is.

John Murray helpfully comments in this regard that the gospel reveals not,

> the bare preceptive will of God but the disposition of lovingkindness on the part of God pointing to the salvation to be gained through compliance with the overtures of gospel grace ... a real attitude, a real disposition of lovingkindness inherent in the free offer to all, in other words, a pleasure or delight in God, contemplating the blessed result to be achieved

by compliance with the overture proffered and the invitation given.[12]

God is not outwardly different in His gospel offer, from what He is in Himself. For all the necessary distinctions we make because of our creatureliness, we must never imagine there is a hidden God of sovereign election to salvation who in some way is different to the compassionate God who calls us to Himself.

More evidence can be produced from other prophets to confirm the same truth, but in conclusion we will just turn to the summary given to us in 2 Chronicles 36:15: 'And the Lord God of their fathers sent *warnings* to them by His messengers, rising up early and sending *them,* because He had compassion on His people and on His dwelling place.' God had sent judgment on Judah. Babylon had laid Jerusalem waste: 'They burned the house of God, broke down the wall of Jerusalem, burned all its palaces with fire, and destroyed all its precious possessions' (2 Chron. 36:19). But this was the result of the spurning of the compassion of God. God had, because of His compassion, sent many prophets to Judah, calling them, pleading with them, to return, warning them of the danger of failing to do God's pleasure. God's desire was that the prophets' message of salvation would have been embraced, that God's call to return to Himself would have been complied with. This is why the gospel came again and again to Israel, to avoid the disaster of judgment. That was God's revealed will, and every expression of the gospel is nothing other than God's compassion.

---

12. John Murray, *Collected Writings*, 4:114.

The Revealed Will and the Gospel in the Gospels

The New Testament is, if anything, clearer than the Old Testament that God wills the salvation of all. We see God's heart for all clearly in the life and ministry of Jesus. We should expect this as Jesus is the one who is 'the exact representation of his being' (Heb. 1:3, NIV). Nowhere do we see Jesus display the Father more clearly than in His laments and tears over Jerusalem (Luke 19:41-42, Matt. 23:37 and Luke 13:34-35).

The emotion that most characterised Jesus' earthly ministry was compassion, overflowing pity when confronted with the misery of sinners. When individuals underwent great suffering, we are often told that Jesus was moved with compassion. To give just one example, in Luke 7 Jesus met a widow whose only son had just died and 'when the Lord saw her, He had compassion on her and said to her, "Do not weep"' (Luke 7:13). Jesus also responded with compassion when He saw great numbers of people in need. In the feeding of the five thousand we read: 'When he went ashore he saw a great crowd, and he had compassion on them, because they were like sheep without a shepherd' (Mark 6:34, ESV). Whether confronted by individual suffering, or by the spiritual blindness of a great crowd, the gospel writers often highlight Jesus' response of compassion.

It is that same compassion that shines through in Jesus' lament over Jerusalem. In Luke 19 Jesus draws near to Jerusalem for the last time. As He sees the city He is profoundly impacted. He sees the city on which God has placed His own name: 'I have chosen Jerusalem, that my name may be there' (2 Chron. 6:6). It was a city God had given so much to. Jerusalem received God's Word, God's love and grace, and God's prophets had ministered to this city for centuries faithfully calling its inhabitants to love God and serve Him. This is the city where the temple and the sacrifices were, with all they pointed to regarding God's presence and His atoning mercy. As Jesus sees this city spread out before him, 'he wept over it' (Luke 19:41). Jesus, knowing that this city will gladly and wilfully put Him to death crying out, 'His blood *be* on us and on our children' (Matt. 27:25), weeps tears of compassion over it. Jesus here weeps for those who would not weep for themselves. This is the city who killed the prophets and stoned the messengers sent to her, and who would now kill the Son of God (Matt. 23:37). But over her, Jesus sheds tears.

This shows us the heart of Jesus towards all. If Jesus weeps tears over unbelieving Jerusalem, it is clear that Jesus' compassion extends to every man, woman and child. Jesus weeps here over the worst sinners of His day, sinners worse than those in Sodom and Gomorrah (Matt. 11:23-24), sinners against light and against knowledge. Over them, yes them, Jesus sheds tears. Here truly is the man who is not willing that any should perish, but that all should come to repentance.

However, Jesus' tears of compassion are not the tears of a mere man. The tears of Jesus are human tears, but they reveal God's attitude of compassion to all, even hardened sinners. Here we have a profound insight into divine benevolence and pity. These tears show us the compassion of God for a world lost in sin. We cannot, and must not, imagine that here the will of the human nature is at variance with the will of the divine nature of the Son – or worse, that the will of the Son is at variance with the will of the Father and the Spirit. John Murray rightly points out, 'we must not fail to keep in mind the principle... [of] the perfect harmony and coalescence of will on the part of the Father and of the Son (cf. John 12:49, 50; 14:10, 24; 17:8). To aver that Jesus in the expressed will of Matthew 23:37 [and Luke 19:41] is not disclosing the *divine* will but simply his own human will would tend towards very grave prejudice to this principle.'[13] The tears are properly the tears of a man, but they express the heart of the Son, and because they do, they reveal the heart of our triune God, the heart of a God who says, 'He had one left to send, a son, whom he loved. He sent him last of all, saying, They will respect my son' (Mark 12:6, NIV).

Jesus, with tears on His cheeks, goes on to explain the reason for His weeping. He cries out, Luke 19:42 (ESV), 'Would that you, even you, had known on this day the things that make for peace!' How Jesus longs for their salvation! Jesus had invited Jerusalem, 'Come to me all who are weary and heavy laden and I will give you rest' (Matt. 11:28). He had preached, come now just as you are, sinners come, and love, mercy and compassion will meet you. Here He laments over their refusal, showing the reality of His lifelong wish that Jerusalem would turn to Him and live. When Jesus wept at the tomb of Lazarus (John 11:35) those who saw this were brought to say, 'See how He loved him!' (John 11:36). No less do Jesus' tears over Jerusalem show His, and the Father's, love for the unbelieving city. It has helpfully been said: 'It is our happiness to believe that when we see Jesus weeping over Jerusalem, we 'have seen the Father,' we have received an insight into the divine benevolence and pity.'[14]

Jesus' (and the Father's) desire is expressed similarly in Matthew 23:37 (c.f. Luke 13:34-35): 'How often I wanted to gather your children together, as a hen gathers her chicks under *her* wings, but you were not willing!' Jesus laments that, despite His desire to protect the people of Jerusalem, they would not come to Him to have life and safety (John 5:40). The image

---

13. Murray, *Collected Writings*, 4:121.
14. Robert L. Dabney, 'God's Indiscriminate Proposals of Mercy, as Related to his Power, Wisdom and Sincerity' in *Discussions of Robert L. Dabney: Vol. 1, Theological and Evangelical* (Richmond, VA: Whittet & Shepperson, 1890), 308.

of shelter under the wings of a bird is an image drawn from God's protection of His people in Psalm 91:4: 'He shall cover you with His feathers, And under His wings you shall take refuge.' This is a great proof (if one were needed) that Jesus' words here have reference to His divinity. Calvin comments that 'Christ is speaking in the Person of God … these words really belong to his eternal Godhead.'[15] He is wishing, as God the Son, that Jerusalem would be under His saving care. But they will not, and so judgment will come on them with no refuge, for they had rejected the revealed will and desire of God for their salvation. As Robert Murray M'Cheyne said, 'God willeth all men to be saved. I believe there is not one soul that the Saviour does not yearn over as he did over Jerusalem; and the Father says: "O that they had hearkened unto me, and Israel had walked in my ways!"'[16]

Jesus' tears are not the only indication of God's will and desire for the salvation of all. In John 3:17 we are told that 'God did not send His Son into the world to condemn the world, but that the world through Him might be saved.' The mission of Jesus in its proper function is not to bring condemnation but salvation. The impulse behind the gospel offer of Jesus is not to add to anyone's judgment (though that may sadly result) but to bring deliverance. Calvin again is helpful when he says, 'the proper function of the Gospel is always to be distinguished from what we may call its accidental function, which must be imputed to the depravity of men by which life is turned into death.'[17] The same truth is declared in John 12:47: 'I did not come to judge the world but to save the world.'

---

15. Calvin, *Calvin's New Testament Commentaries*, 3:69.
16. Robert Murray M'Cheyne, *From the Preacher's Heart: Additional Remains* (Repr.; Fearn: Christian Focus, 1993), 94.
17. Calvin, *Calvin's New Testament Commentaries*, 10:35.

The willingness of God to save is the clear implication of John 5:40: 'But you are not willing to come to Me that you may have life.' Salvation is there to be received, God is willing to bestow it, and the lack is not in God's willingness but in the willingness of sinners to come to Jesus. This is reinforced in the strength of Jesus' promise: 'the one who comes to Me I will by no means cast out' (John 6:37).

The Revealed Will and the Gospel in the New Testament Epistles

Moving on to the rest of the New Testament, Paul in Romans clearly teaches God's revealed will for the salvation of all, while being equally insistent on the sovereign choice of God in election (Rom. 9:6-33). We see this even in the verses which bookend Paul's exposition of God's decree of predestination. Paul begins Romans 9 by stating:

> I tell the truth in Christ, I am not lying, my conscience also bearing me witness in the Holy Spirit, that I have great sorrow and continual grief in my heart. For I could wish that I myself were accursed from Christ for my brethren, my countrymen according to the flesh. (Rom. 9:1-3)

Paul is shaken to his core in grief and sorrow of the rejection of the gospel by Israel. He goes on to show this is all under the sovereign will of God, but this does not prevent his heartbreak over this state of affairs. So great is his grief that he even says he could forego his own salvation for their eternal good. After underlining that sovereignty of God, Paul returns to this theme saying, 'Brethren, my heart's desire and prayer to God for Israel is that they may be saved' (Rom. 10:1). In all this Paul was following in the footsteps of his Lord and God, who, as we have seen, wept Himself over lost sinners and ultimately experienced darkness and forsakenness (Matt. 27:45-46) that the gospel might go to all the nations.

Now, what are we to make of Paul's sorrow? Of the desire in his heart to pray for the salvation of Israel? Where did the sorrow of heart and prayer come from? Were they not inspired by the Spirit? Were they not consistent with the pleasure and desire of God? Yes, by the very nature of the case they must be. But again, we aren't left to the deductions of our own logic. Paul tells us that his longings are patterned after the longings of God. He goes on to tell us that it is not just him who desires Israel's salvation, but God. This desire of God is shown in the posture He adopts to His reprobate people: 'All day long I have stretched out My hands To a disobedient and contrary people' (Rom. 10:21, c.f. Isa. 65:2). The Lord is like a father waiting for the return of His prodigal child (Luke 15:11-32), longing for their return. God waits with stretched out hands to Israel, who repeatedly rejected this offered love. As Charles Hodge says, 'God's dealings even with reprobate sinners, are full of tenderness and compassion. All the day long he extends the arms of his mercy, even to the disobedient and gainsaying.'[18] God, Paul is clear, *wants* the salvation of those who reject Him.

We see this again in Paul's conception of gospel ministry. We have turned to this verse a few times because of the structurally important place it has in understanding the gospel offer. But consider again Paul's image for gospel ministers in 2 Corinthians 5:20: 'Now then, we are ambassadors for Christ, as though God were pleading through us: we implore *you* on Christ's behalf, be reconciled to God.' What is important in this image is God's pleading. Here is the sovereign, eternal, ever blessed God pleading with His creatures to accept His offered salvation and to apply to themselves the great truth that 'He made Him who knew no sin *to be* sin for us, that we might become the righteousness of God

---

18. Hodge, *Romans*, 352.

in Him' (2 Cor. 5:21). Now, why would God plead with sinners to do something He didn't want? Obviously, He wouldn't. God is pleading with all sinners to accept the gospel because He wants them to, because He desires them to. It is pleasing to God that sinners receive Jesus freely offered in the gospel, so pleasing that He pleads with them to do that.

There are two other verses in the New Testament which also teach this clearly, 1 Timothy 2:4 and 2 Peter 3:9. In 1 Timothy 2 Paul has been teaching that 'supplications, prayers, intercessions, *and* giving of thanks be made for all men' and in particular for those in authority (1 Tim. 2:1-2). Why should we pray for all? Because, Paul says, God 'desires all men to be saved and to come to the knowledge of the truth' (1 Tim. 2:4). God's revealed will for all to be saved, God's pleasure in the salvation of sinners, is the impelling motive for our prayers for all. This salvation which God wills for all is only to be found in the one all sufficient sacrifice of Jesus Christ (1 Tim. 2:5-6). We are to pray that all will come to know this salvation, because it is pleasing to our God. Peter brings the same truth before us in 2 Peter 3:9: 'The Lord is not slack concerning *His* promise, as some count slackness, but is longsuffering toward us, not willing that any should perish but that all should come to repentance.' The background here is impatience for the return of the Lord Jesus. Peter reminds his readers that this delay is not without purpose. It reveals the great truth that God is 'longsuffering toward us, not willing that any should perish but that all should come to repentance.' This refers to all the people mentioned in the surrounding passage by Peter (scoffers, those who perished in the flood etc.), and by extension to all people. The Bible is clear that God's longsuffering extends to everyone (Rom. 2:4). This longsuffering has the purpose of revealing God's willingness for all to repent. Why else should time be given to sinners before their judgment except to give them opportunity to repent, and to reveal God's unwillingness that they should be lost? Indeed, Calvin tells us that this verse shows us God's 'wondrous love towards the human race' expressing itself in a 'desire that all men be saved'.[19]

This same unwillingness for sinners to be lost is seen in Revelation 3:20. As has been demonstrated before this verse is addressed to many unbelievers. What posture does God adopt towards them? The posture of one desiring admittance into their hearts: 'Behold, I stand at the door and knock. If anyone hears My voice and opens the door, I will come in to him and dine with him, and he with Me' (Rev. 3:20). Why does someone knock at the door? One reason is because they want to come inside. They have an offer to make and want an answer. It is exactly so in the gospel. The Lord wants every heart which hears the gospel to open to Him. He desires to come in and enjoy saving fellowship with all sinners. James Durham helpfully paraphrased Revelation 3:20 as follows: 'I come in my gospel to woo, and, if any will consent to take me on the terms on which I offer myself, I will be theirs.'[20]

Conclusion

This is the burden of the gospel. Yes, God wants you to accept the gospel, 'Christ is willing to come into every heart. Why else does he demand open doors, but because he is willing to enter.'[21] It is His great pleasure that any and all sinners receive salvation in His Son. For, 'I tell you, there is rejoicing in the presence of the angels of God over one sinner who repents' (Luke 15:10, NIV). It is not, for His own good and wise reasons, His decree that all will be saved, but the salvation of any and all sinners is a thing that He delights in.

---

19. Calvin, *Calvin's New Testament Commentaries*, 12:364.
20. Durham, *Unsearchable Riches*, 46.
21. Boston, *Works*, 3:102-3.

7

THE GOSPEL –
GRACE AND LOVE TO ALL?

*Cannot God have compassion even on the condemned sinner,
and bestow favours upon him? ... Prov. 1:24; Isa. 1:18; Ezek.
18:23,32; 33:11; Matt. 5:43-45; 23:37; Mark. 10:21; Luke
6:35; Rom. 2:4; 1 Tim. 2:4. If such passages do not testify to
a favourable disposition in God [to all], it would seem that
language has lost its meaning...*
Louis Berkhof (1873-1957)[1]

Related to the question of whether God wills for all to accept
the gospel, is the question of whether God shows grace to all
and loves all. A nuanced answer is needed. God shows common
grace to all, and loves all with a common love. However, He
shows special saving grace and love only to His chosen people.
It is only God's people who can say, 'But God, who is rich
in mercy, because of His great love with which He loved us,
even when we were dead in trespasses, made us alive together
with Christ (by grace you have been saved)' (Eph. 2:4-5). John
Murray cautions that 'we must jealously guard the distinction
between the grace that is common and the grace that is saving.'[2]

---

1. Berkhof, *Systematic Theology*, 445-6.
2. Murray, *Collected Writings*, 2:117.

ALL THINGS ARE READY

Granting this, the burden of this chapter is not to expound this special grace and love but to demonstrate that God shows common grace and love to all, and that one expression of that love and grace is the gospel invitation. Every individual is able to say that they are loved by God, that they experience God's love and that God's love in all its fullness is offered to them in the gospel (John 3:16).

God Is Good to All

Grace in its essence is unmerited favour. However, after the fall of humanity into sin, any goodness God bestows is not simply unmerited favour, but favour in the face of de-merit. No one deserves anything good. Everyone deserves the eternal wrath of God against their sin. That God instead deals with the world so much better than any deserve is an expression of grace. As Louis Berkhof outlines, '[God] could not be good, kind, or benevolent to the *sinner* unless he were first of all *gracious*.'[3]

We see this in the early days of post-fall history. In Genesis 4 we have a record of the great sin of Cain, in murdering his brother Abel (Gen. 4:8). But there is also great common grace. Cain is spared the punishment he deserves (death), with God even protecting him (Gen. 4:15). More than this, we see how God blesses Cain's descendants. It is through them that animal husbandry developed (Gen. 4:20), that music flowered (Gen. 4:21) and through whom technological advances were made (Gen. 4:22). These are good things in themselves, 'the riches of his favour' which the line of Cain does not deserve.[4] They are fruits of God's grace, even to a people who will ultimately abuse

---

3. Berkhof, *Systematic Theology*, 435.
4. John Calvin, *Genesis* (Trans. John King; 2 vols. in 1; repr.; Edinburgh: Banner of Truth, 1984), 1:218.

them as they degenerate into the wicked condition that leads to the judgment of the flood (Gen. 6:7).

It is after the flood that we see one of the richest fruits of common grace, the covenant with Noah. Upon leaving the ark, Noah offered a sacrifice to God. And following this, 'The Lord said in His heart, I will never again curse the ground for man's sake, although the imagination of man's heart *is* evil from his youth; nor will I again destroy every living thing as I have done. While the earth remains, Seedtime and harvest, Cold and heat, Winter and summer, And day and night Shall not cease' (Gen. 8:21-22). The result of this purpose of God was a covenant which would be made with the whole earth:

> And as for Me, behold, I establish My covenant with you and with your descendants after you, and with every living creature that *is* with you: the birds, the cattle, and every beast of the earth with you, of all that go out of the ark, every beast of the earth. Thus I establish My covenant with you: Never again shall all flesh be cut off by the waters of the flood; never again shall there be a flood to destroy the earth (Gen. 9:9-11).

Instead of the judgment of another flood, there would be the blessing of seasons, of sowing and reaping, of the rhythms of life. God sealed this promise with the covenant sign of the rainbow, so that any time that the rainbow was seen it would be a token to the world of God's covenanted goodness and faithfulness (Gen. 9:12-17). It is impossible to restrict this covenant to any one group of individuals. Noah is the new Adam in the sense that all humanity flows from him. As such, everyone is in the category of 'your descendants after you'. The covenant with Noah seals God's common blessings and grace to all humanity.

We see this clearly proclaimed in the Psalms. Psalm 33:5 tells us that 'The earth is full of the goodness of the Lord' or 'full of his unfailing love' (NIV). God goes beyond not doing the world any wrong, He positively fills the world with His kindness, mercy, love and common grace. Nor can the scope of this goodness be limited for the Psalm goes on to call all in the earth to serve God: 'Let all the earth fear the Lord; Let all the inhabitants of the world stand in awe of Him' (Ps. 33:8). As Calvin comments we see in here that 'the benefits of God which he scatters over the whole human race ... meet us wherever we turn our eyes.'[5] We see the same truth in Psalm 104:14-15 where some of the blessings that are poured out on humanity are listed for us: 'He causes the grass to grow for the cattle, And vegetation for the service of man, That he may bring forth food from the earth, And wine *that* makes glad the heart of man, Oil to make *his* face shine, And bread *which* strengthens man's heart.' Food, wine, oil, bread, all these things are gifts of God's common grace to the world and bring gladness to the heart (Ps. 4:7). Psalm 136:25 specifically tells us that these are a gift of God's grace: 'Who gives food to all flesh, For His mercy *endures* forever.' It is through God's common mercy that the creation produces food for us. Any doubt on this is put away by Psalm 145:8-9: 'The Lord *is* gracious and full of compassion, Slow to anger and great in mercy. The Lord *is* good to all, And His tender mercies *are* over all His works.' (Or 'slow to anger and rich in love', NIV.) It is this unchanging and unchangeable character of God as gracious, compassionate and longsuffering that causes Him to be good to His fallen world and show it mercy. Even in something as seemingly mundane as giving 'food in due season' we see that 'the Lord *is* ... Gracious in all His works' (Ps. 145:15-17, c.f. Ps. 65:9-13).

The New Testament likewise insists that God is gracious to all. In Matthew 5:44-45 and Luke 6:27-36 we are clearly told God blesses *all* of humanity, and therefore we are to do likewise. We are called in Matthew 5:44 to 'bless' and 'do good' to those who are our enemies, and who do us harm. The basis

---

5.   Calvin, *Calvin's Commentaries*, 4:542.

for this is that God does these things to His enemies (Matt. 5:48). Luke is even clearer; he explicitly records that God is 'kind to the unthankful and evil' (Luke. 6:35). We will return to these passages again shortly.

Paul also is clear that God is good to all. He asks, 'Or do you despise the riches of His goodness, forbearance, and longsuffering, not knowing that the goodness of God leads you to repentance?' (Rom 2:4). The point is that God must show His grace to all, for them to be able to learn repentance from it. The fruits of common grace (goodness, patience, longsuffering) reach to all. The goodness of God should be sufficient of itself to lead to a turning to God. The tendency inherent in it is to produce a change of heart, were it not for the spiritual blindness of the world.

Paul preached the same truths in Acts. At Lystra he proclaimed that, even while the gospel was treasured only in Israel, the common grace of God revealed the reality of His being to the rest of the world, for 'He did not leave Himself without witness, in that He did good, gave us rain from heaven and fruitful seasons, filling our hearts with food and gladness' (Acts. 14:17). He did good to all, throughout the history of the fallen world.

God's common grace is shown then in His super-abounding all-encompassing goodness. Truly, 'every good gift and every perfect gift is from above, and comes down from the Father of lights' (James 1:17). Every good thing in this world is a gift of common grace from the God 'who richly provides us with everything for our enjoyment' (1 Tim. 6:17, NIV).

God Restrains Sin and Empowers Good Works

As well as doing good to all, God's common grace is evident in His restraining sin and wickedness. This world is fallen in sin, but it is far from as bad as it could be. Positively there are many people who do 'good' works. This is all of God's grace. The history recounted in Genesis 20 reflects both of these aspects. Here Abraham has fallen into sin. In fear he had refused to own Sarah as his wife, and so she has been taken by Abimelech the king of Gerar to be his wife. But God warned Abimelech in a dream that Sarah was truly Abraham's wife. This struck fear into Abimelech's heart, but God said to him, 'Yes, I know that you did this in the integrity of your heart. For I also withheld you from sinning against Me; therefore I did not let you touch her' (Gen. 20:6). God acknowledged the righteous behaviour of Abimelech. In this whole sad affair, though we have no reason to suppose he had faith in God, he acted with 'integrity' – a character trait he would not have had as a fallen sinner apart from God's grace (c.f. Ps. 14:1-3). And again, we see God's active role in restraining sin. God prevented Abimelech from consummating the relationship with Sarah. God, in grace, kept a bad situation from becoming worse. Here we have 'an unbeliever restrained by divine intervention from the commission of sin'.[6]

This sin-restraining work of the Spirit of God (even among unbelievers) can be seen in various passages of scripture. Genesis 6:3 tells us that 'My Spirit shall not strive with man forever'. This is a clear revelation that God's Spirit was at work in the days before the flood, preventing sin becoming worse. Isaiah 63:10 tells us how Israel in the wilderness 'rebelled and grieved His Holy Spirit' until He became their enemy. Again,

---

6. Murray, *Collected Writings*, 2:100.

it is clear that the Spirit was at work restraining their sin, until their rejection of His common grace became so egregious that He left them to themselves. A similar point is made by Stephen in Acts 7:51 in his address before the Sanhedrin: '*You* stiff-necked and uncircumcised in heart and ears! You always resist the Holy Spirit; as your fathers *did,* so *do* you.' The Spirit was at work, in common grace restraining their sin, but they rebelled against this. As Charles Hodge writes, 'The Spirit, therefore, is represented as striving with the wicked, and with all men. They are charged with resisting, grieving, vexing and quenching his operations. This is the familiar mode of Scriptural representation.'[7]

God's restraint of sin can be seen in the impact of His withdrawal of His Spirit. This is perhaps seen best in the case of King Saul. Because of Saul's sin, we read 'the Spirit of the Lord departed from Saul' and in its place 'a harmful spirit from the Lord tormented him' (1 Sam. 16:14, ESV). Now there is much that is difficult here. But what is clear is that at one time God's Spirit worked in Saul, restraining him from sin and doing him good. That common grace was received in vain, and so God gave Saul up to evil. This shows that common grace is not equally given to all, or even to the same individual in the same measure all their days. Much the same could be said of Pharaoh. God's giving Pharaoh over to the hardness of his own heart (e.g. Exod. 8:15, 32; 9:34), and in doing so hardening his heart (Exod. 9:12; 10:1, 20, 27; 11:10; 14:4, 8, 17), implies that before this He was restraining Pharaoh's wickedness, showing him common grace in keeping him from being as bad as otherwise he might be.

God also uses other means under common grace to restrain evil. The institution of government is one of these. Paul tells

---

7. Charles Hodge, *Systematic Theology* (3 vols.; repr., Peabody, MA: Hendrickson Publishers, 2003), 2:668.

in in Romans 13:1-2 that He has ordained the governing authorities. The role God has given them is to encourage good and punish evil: 'Do you want to be unafraid of the authority? Do what is good, and you will have praise from the same. For he is God's minister to you for good. But if you do evil, be afraid; for he does not bear the sword in vain' (Rom. 13:3-4). Government is for our good. It is a gift of God. Yes, it can be abused (and it was in Paul's day) but its tendency is to provide order and be a blessing in God's common grace. This is what Peter says as well in 1 Peter 2:14: 'Governors ... are sent by him for the punishment of evildoers and *for the* praise of those who do good.'

But as well as restraining sin, God in common grace enables fallen men and women to do good. Now, this is not to say that absolute good is done, for 'There is none who does good, no, not one' (Rom. 3:12). But the Bible is clear that by common grace the unregenerate can do 'good', where 'good' means works which outwardly are in conformity to God's law (though devoid of heart obedience), indeed, 'the Bible repeatedly speaks of works of the unregenerate as good and right'.[8] As referred to above, Romans 13:3 says 'rulers are not a terror to good works, but to evil'. What does Paul mean by 'good works'? He simply means conformity to God's law in outward actions. This is what rulers are to encourage. It is a 'good work' not to steal, and it is 'evil' to steal. Jesus in Luke talks of 'those who do good to you' (Luke 6:33) who are yet unsaved. The record of the Kings of Israel and Judah is another confirmation that the unsaved can do 'good'. Jehu was a man who 'took no heed to walk in the law of the Lord God of Israel with all his heart; for he did not depart from the sins of Jeroboam, who had made Israel sin' (2 Kings 10:31). Nonetheless the Lord said to him, 'Because you have done well in doing *what is* right in My sight, *and*

---

8. Berkhof, *Systematic Theology*, 443.

have done to the house of Ahab all that *was* in My heart, your sons shall sit on the throne of Israel to the fourth *generation*' (2 Kings 10:30). Though an unsaved man, he is one whom God recognises has done good, and so receives a temporal reward. Here is common grace, here is God rewarding and recognising the fruit of His own non-saving work. We cannot deny that 'good is attributed to unregenerate men.'[9]

God Loves All

Now why does God show favour to all? Why does He restrain sin and inspire good works? Because He loves all His creatures. This is the simple and beautiful teaching of Matthew 5:44-48 and Luke 6:27-36. Matthew records Jesus exhorting His disciples to 'love your enemies, bless those who curse you, do good to those who hate you, and pray for those who spitefully use you and persecute you' (Matt. 5:44). They are to love those who do not love them, even their enemies. And they are to show this by 'doing good' towards those who show them only hate. Now why are they to do this? So that 'you may be sons of your Father in heaven; for He makes His sun rise on the evil and on the good, and sends rain on the just and on the unjust' (Matt. 5:45). The disciples are called to love their enemies that they might share in the family resemblance of the Father. He is the archetype of one who loves His enemies. He is the one who shows His love by doing good to those who hate Him. He has given them the blessing (while they curse Him!) of sun and rain, the bounty of nature: 'goodness and beneficence, kindness and mercy are here attributed to God in his relations even to the ungodly.'[10] This divine kindness is a manifestation of nothing other than divine love. If we are to be 'perfect, just

9. Murray, *Collected Writings*, 2:106.
10. Murray, *Collected Writings*, 2:105.

as your Father in heaven is perfect' then we must do likewise (Matt. 5:48). If we do not, if we only love those who love us, we are like the 'tax collectors' rather than God (Matt. 5:46).

Luke's account drives this same point home, as Jesus is recorded saying, 'But love your enemies, do good, and lend, hoping for nothing in return; and your reward will be great, and you will be sons of the Most High. For He is kind to the unthankful and evil. Therefore be merciful, just as your Father also is merciful.' (Luke 6:35-36). Again, the exhortation is to love our enemies that we might show our likeness to our Father. But the link here is more explicit. Luke says that God is 'kind to the unthankful and evil'. He is benevolent to those who are utterly undeserving. And because of this loving act of God, 'Therefore be merciful, just as your Father also is merciful.' Because of who God is in Himself, and how He therefore acts, we are to show mercy to all. In this we imitate the Father's universal mercy and love.

God therefore loves all, and this is the basis for our love to all. Now we have to remember crucial distinctions when discussing the love of God. Jesus has a special love for His Church, His saved people (Eph. 5:25). It cannot be said of all that 'In love he predestined us for adoption to sonship through Jesus Christ, in accordance with his pleasure and will' (Eph. 1:4-5, NIV). But besides this special love for His chosen people, God has a general love for all. This is expressed in His kindness to all, and as will now be seen, the gospel invitation is one important aspect of that kindness.

God's Gospel Shows Common Grace and Universal Love (The Old Testament Witness)

In one sense it is obvious that if gifts like sun, rain, food and so on show God's common grace and love then the wonderful gospel invitation must as well. It is a greater spiritual blessing to have the bread of life offered to an individual than for them to have daily bread. To have the good news preached to an individual is a great kindness, and it must, as such, flow from the mercy and love of God. But again, we do not have to rely on inference. The Bible clearly links the gospel invitation to the kindness and grace of God.

In Genesis we see examples of how being in the sphere of gospel privileges brought blessings. In Genesis 17:20 we are told how Ishmael, although ultimately to be 'cast out' (Gen. 21:10), was none the less blessed. In response to Abraham, God said, 'As for Ishmael, I have heard you. Behold, I have blessed him, and will make him fruitful, and will multiply him exceedingly' (Gen. 21:20). Ishmael was circumcised (Gen. 17:26), a token of gospel privilege (Rom. 4:11), and though he would not be heir of the ultimate covenant promises (Gen. 17:21) he was the recipient of divine blessing. This was all in connection with Abraham as the father of the faithful. Because of this connection Ishmael had to the gospel (sealed in circumcision) he received temporal blessings from God. His connection with the gospel brought him common grace.

We see something similar in connection with the life of Joseph. Joseph has been sold by his brothers into slavery in Egypt. He has been 'bought' by 'Potiphar, an officer of Pharaoh, captain of the guard, an Egyptian' (Gen. 39:1). But in that terrible condition of slavery God was kind to Joseph and made him successful, so much so that Potiphar put his household under Joseph's authority. Now, Joseph was God's saviour for the world in these days. Joseph was the one who through his own sufferings would save Egypt and the surrounding countries from disaster under famine. Being near to one who in many ways foreshadows Jesus and who would become Egypt's saviour was a gospel privilege for Potiphar, for Joseph was a witness to him. In this he was blessed, as we read, 'The Lord blessed the Egyptian's house for Joseph's sake; and the blessing of the Lord was on all that he had in the house and in the field' (Gen. 39:5). Again, here is common grace in connection with gospel privilege. Potiphar is blessed through his connection with Joseph.

But as we go on through scripture, we see deeper and more profound blessings accompanying the gospel. We have revealed for us a love from God that goes beyond the general love that He shows all His creatures, a love specifically shown in connection with the gospel (but which still falls short of effectual saving love). We see this in Moses' teaching in Deuteronomy. Repeatedly God tells Israel that He loves them as His 'special treasure above all the peoples on the face of the earth' (Deut. 7:6). We are told that God led Israel out of Egypt because He loved them: 'The Lord loves you, and because He would keep the oath which He swore to your fathers, the Lord has brought you out with a mighty hand, and redeemed you from the house of bondage, from the hand of Pharaoh king of Egypt' (Deut. 7:8). We are told He delivered them from curses because He loved them: 'The Lord your God turned the curse into a blessing for you, because the Lord your God loves you' (Deut. 23:5). We are told that God gave them the Ten Commandments because He loved them: 'The Lord came from Sinai … From His right hand *Came* a fiery law for them. Yes, He loves the people … *Everyone* receives Your words. Moses commanded a law for us, A heritage of the congregation of Jacob' (Deut. 33:2-4).

Now, were all Israel loved by God savingly? No. In fact we know that the vast majority of Israel were unbelievers who died in their sins. Those God loved enough to redeem from Egypt, those God loved enough to give His word at Sinai, mostly rejected their covenant God. Hebrews 3:16-19 reflects:

For who, having heard, rebelled? Indeed, *was it* not all who came out of Egypt, *led* by Moses? Now with whom was He angry forty years? *Was it* not with those who sinned, whose corpses fell in the wilderness? And to whom did He swear that they would not enter His rest, but to those who did not obey? So we see that they could not enter in because of unbelief.

But God tells us He loved those same individuals. And that love included giving them the gospel: 'Indeed the gospel was preached to us as well as to them; but the word which they heard did not profit them, not being mixed with faith in those who heard *it*' (Heb. 4:2). Even more, in giving them the gospel, God was giving them Christ. As Paul says, the Israelites in the wilderness 'drank of that spiritual Rock that followed them, and that Rock was Christ' (1 Cor. 10:4). However, they were not saved, for 'with most of them God was not well pleased, for *their bodies* were scattered in the wilderness' (1 Cor. 10:5). God loved Israel as He gave them the gospel of His Son, but He did not save them. This tells us there is a grace and love that accompanies the gospel specifically, which though it falls short of saving love, is nonetheless real divine love.

Calvin echoed this teaching in preaching on Deuteronomy 4:37 (particularly the phrase 'because He loved your fathers'). He said that in addition to the saving love of God there was a love 'which extendeth to all men, inasmuch as Jesus Christ reacheth out his arms to call and allure all men, both great and small, and to win them to him' and a 'special love' (but still not saving) which was evident towards those 'to whom the gospel is preached'.[11]

Other Old Testament passages reinforce this common grace and love in connection with the gospel. Psalm 78 reflects

---

11. Calvin, *Sermons on Deuteronomy*, 167.

on Israel's unfaithfulness after being redeemed from Egypt, and God's continual response of mercy and kindness. Israel's behaviour can be summed up as: 'Their heart was not steadfast with Him, Nor were they faithful in His covenant' (Ps. 78:37). And yet to these people who 'tested God again and again' (Ps. 78:41, ESV), 'He, *being* full of compassion, forgave *their* iniquity, And did not destroy *them*. Yes, many a time He turned His anger away, And did not stir up all His wrath' (Ps. 78:38). To a people who rejected Him, God showed mercy, compassion and forgiveness enough to refrain from temporal punishments.

Again, in the Levites' reflection in Nehemiah 9 on the history of Israel's rebellion, we see God's non-saving love and kindness displayed. Israel are described as those who 'acted presumptuously' who 'stiffened their neck' and who 'did not obey your commandments' to the extent that they 'appointed a leader to return to their slavery in Egypt' (Neh. 9:16-17, ESV). Yet to this reprobate people, God showed Himself to be 'a God ready to forgive, gracious and merciful, slow to anger and abounding in steadfast love' (Neh. 9:17, ESV). Common grace and love, were poured out on an unsaved and ungrateful people to such an extent that even when they worshipped the golden calf as the God who redeemed them from Egypt, 'you in your great mercies did not forsake them in the wilderness' (Neh. 9:19, ESV). This pattern of love and grace shown to an unthankful people was repeated through Israel's history:

> According to your great mercies you gave them saviours who saved them from the hand of their enemies ... many times you delivered them according to your mercies. And you warned them in order to turn them back to your law. Yet they acted presumptuously and did not obey your commandments ... Many years you bore with them and warned them by your Spirit through your prophets. Yet they would not give ear. (Neh. 9:27-30, ESV)

All through Israel's history, offers of gospel forgiveness showed them God's love, and His patient dealings in restraining judgment showed them His mercy and grace. Also, wherever there is a suspension of judgment, whether before the flood (1 Pet. 3:20), whether for Israel (Luke 13:6-9), or for the world today (2 Pet. 3:9) this is an expression of God's common grace and love restraining His judgment.

Why, though, does God generally mercifully delay judgment? Because, as Isaiah 28:21 tells us, it is His 'strange work' (KJV), 'unusual act' or 'alien act' (NIV). Judgment is, as it were, forced from God, while mercy and grace flow freely. God, as we have seen, does not afflict willingly nor grieve the children of men from His heart (Lam. 3:33). God's character, His attributes, have a predisposition to keeping mercy. He is first 'The Lord, the Lord God, merciful and gracious, longsuffering, and abounding in goodness and truth, keeping mercy for thousands, forgiving iniquity and transgression and sin' and only then is He the one who 'by no means clears *the guilty*' (Exod. 34:6-7, ESV). Our God 'delights *in* mercy' (Micah 7:18).

It is because of who God is that we can 'mention the lovingkindnesses of the Lord … And the great goodness toward the house of Israel, Which He has bestowed on them according to His mercies, According to the multitude of His lovingkindnesses' (Isa. 63:7). God's merciful character causes Him to show this love and mercy to a people who 'rebelled and grieved His Holy Spirit' and ultimately in their stubborn disobedience against gospel privileges and love caused God to 'turn Himself against them as an enemy' (Isa. 63:10). Throughout the life of God's chosen nation of Israel: 'they mocked the messengers of God, despised His words, and scoffed at His prophets, until the wrath of the Lord arose against His people, till *there was* no remedy' (2 Chron. 36:16). But this was not for a lack of gospel love and grace showed to them in the gospel: 'The Lord God of their fathers sent *warnings* to them by His messengers, rising up early and sending *them,* because He had compassion on His people' (2 Chron. 36:15).

One other (and final) example of common grace, mercy and love in connection with the gospel in the Old Testament is found in Hosea. In his prophecy, Hosea (the name means salvation) warned the people of Israel that their sins against God's steadfast covenant love would lead to judgment, but that even in that judgment God's love stood firm. Chapter 11 gives us a wonderful image to understand this, that of a father and a child. God tells us that 'When Israel *was* a child, I loved him' and that as a result of this God both saved them from Egypt ('out of Egypt I called My son') and cared for them as a gentle and kind parent would ('I taught Ephraim to walk, Taking them by their arms', Hosea 11:1-3). However, despite God's loving dealing with His people ('I drew them with gentle cords, With bands of love,' Hosea 11:4), they rejected Him. Calvin notes that 'God had laid on the people ... a certain and singular token of his paternal favour' saying 'I indeed wished to do them good' but 'such kindness had no influence over them'.[12] Instead of responding to His love 'They sacrificed to the Baals, And burned incense to carved images' such that God had to say, 'My people are bent on backsliding from Me' (Hosea 11:2, 7). God uses astonishing language to express the reluctance of His judgment on them for despising His love and blessings: 'How can I give you up, Ephraim? *How* can I hand you over, Israel? ... My heart churns within Me; My sympathy is stirred' (Hosea 11:8). The reality of the genuineness of God's grace and love is shown here. His heart and His sympathy are for Israel, even as they are to suffer judgment for their sins. There is perfect sincerity in God's love, even when it is despised.

---

12. Calvin, *Calvin's Commentaries*, 13:392-3.

God in love gave His people everything (c.f. Ezek. 16:8-14). Their rejection of God was a sin against love and grace.

Israel, then, received (non-saving) love and grace in connection with the gospel. To have this was a blessing from God: 'What advantage then has the Jew, or what *is* the profit of circumcision? Much in every way! Chiefly because to them were committed the oracles of God' (Rom. 3:1-2) They were advantaged by God's goodness and mercy to them, and their unfaithfulness did not nullify the kindness of God to them. God's love remained a good thing for them, despite their rejection of it: 'For what if some did not believe? Will their unbelief make the faithfulness of God without effect? Certainly not! Indeed, let God be true but every man a liar' (Rom. 3:3-4).

God's Gospel Shows Common Grace and Universal Love (The New Testament Witness)

The Lord Jesus connects His own gospel appeals with a love to the unsaved. In Mark 10:17-22 Jesus brings the gospel before a man lost in self-righteousness. Jesus was walking along a road when suddenly a figure comes running up to Him and asks 'Good Teacher, what shall I do that I may inherit eternal life?' (Mark. 10:17). Jesus first points the man to the law, with the purpose of getting him to see his sins. But he is undaunted before the Ten Commandments and the reply comes back: 'Teacher, all these things I have kept from my youth' (Mark. 10:20). How does Jesus respond to such self-righteousness? He responds in love: 'Jesus, looking at him, loved him' (Mark. 10:21). Jesus demonstrates that love in trying to show the man his sins that he might value and embrace the gospel. He says to him, 'One thing you lack: Go your way, sell whatever you have and give to the poor … come, take up the cross, and follow Me' (Mark. 10:21). But this loving appeal to leave self-righteousness

133

and embrace Jesus was rejected, as 'he was sad at this word, and went away sorrowful, for he had great possessions' (Mark. 10:22). We hear no more of this individual. Having rejected the Jesus who loves him he disappears from the narrative. But that does not detract from the genuineness of Jesus' love and compassion (c.f. Matt. 9:36, 14:14, 15:32). Despite being unsaved, Jesus still loved him.

We also see in the Gospels that the gospel offer is intended (in the sense of the revealed will) to save those to whom it comes, unless they twist it to their own loss. In Luke 7:29-30 we are told that 'the tax collectors justified God, having been baptised with the baptism of John. But the Pharisees and lawyers rejected the will of God for themselves, not having been baptised by him.' The gospel was preached even to the Pharisees, with the native intent and purpose of salvation. But they 'rejected God's purpose for themselves' (Luke 7:30, NIV) in refusing to embrace the gospel. God was saying, 'I would have healed Israel' (Hosea 7:1), but the Pharisees refused to be healed.

Both these thoughts (divine love and a native tendency in the gospel to save) are brought together in perhaps the most famous 'gospel offer' in the Bible, John 3:16-17:

> For God so loved the world that He gave His only begotten Son, that whoever believes in Him should not perish but have everlasting life. For God did not send His Son into the world to condemn the world, but that the world through Him might be saved.

Here we are told that God's love for the world results in the gospel offer of eternal life in Jesus Christ. From God's love in giving His Son flows the universal 'that whoever believes in Him should not perish but have everlasting life'. The 'world' here cannot be restricted to a group representing some subset within the broader world, such as the elect or the saved. If the world here meant 'the elect' John would hardly have to clarify that Jesus did not come into the world to condemn *them* (John 3:17). More than that, we know that the world here is broader than those saved, for, 'the light has come into the world, and men loved darkness rather than light, because their deeds were evil' (John 3:19). So, because the world is broader than the saved, it is right to see the love in John 3:16 as the giving love shown in the gospel offer. The love that goes to all the world, is the love that says, 'whoever believes in Him should not perish but have everlasting life'. Thomas Manton rightly says that the world of John 3:16 is 'mankind in its corrupt and miserable state' and to this world God shows 'the love of benevolence ... pity and compassion ... towards man lying in sin'.[13]

John 3:17 goes on to confirm this understanding. As it explicates the teaching that God loved the world we are told that 'God did not send His Son into the world to condemn the world'. This is deeply surprising. The world is sunk in sin, it is anti-God (Rom. 1:18-32), and it deserves condemnation. But that is not why Jesus comes to anyone in the gospel offer. Rather, Jesus comes 'that the world through Him might be saved' (see also Matthew 21:37). The world is condemned already (John 3:18-20). It does not need to be condemned; it needs to be saved. That is the revealed purpose of Christ's coming to sinners in the gospel. It isn't the loving offer of Jesus that condemns anyone, but unbelief and contempt of Christ. Though Jesus' coming will ultimately result in condemnation (John 9:39), it is first true that 'I did not come to judge the world but to save the world' (John 12:47). Jesus came in love to invite the world to receive peace and mercy, to invite them to believe and be saved. That is the great message of John 3:16-17.

---

13. Manton, *Works*, 2:340.

Other New Testament passages also show that the gospel offer is an expression of grace and love. We have considered the gospel invitation in 2 Cor. 5:20 at several points: 'We implore *you* on Christ's behalf, be reconciled to God'. Paul goes on to say to the Corinthians: 'We then, *as* workers together *with Him* also plead with *you* not to receive the grace of God in vain' (2 Cor. 6:1). Paul (together with Christ) sees the gospel invitation as an expression of grace and calls on the Corinthians not to reject and despise the grace of the gospel offer, and so receive it in vain. The gospel offer is given that sinners would come to Christ. To reject it, is to make it 'vain'. Paul also calls the gospel offer 'grace' in Titus 2:11, where he says 'the grace of God has appeared that offers salvation to all people' (NIV). The gospel is grace for all. And it is for all because, 'the living God ... is *the* Saviour of all men, especially of those who believe' (1 Tim. 4:10). Jesus is the Saviour of the world by office. He is offered to all. All are invited and commanded to take Him as their redeemer. All have this kindness and grace shown to them, but those who believe have full saving love of grace shown to them.

These common blessings from God are not only a great blessing; they also bring great responsibility: 'for everyone to whom much is given, from him much will be required; and to whom much has been committed, of him they will ask the more' (Luke 12:48). Just as Israel in the Old Testament was ultimately judged for their sins against God's love, those who receive love and grace in connection with the gospel offer will receive judgment if they reject Jesus. Hebrews 6 outlines the effects of common grace which includes a level of spiritual enlightenment, tasting something of Jesus, becoming a 'partaker of the Holy Spirit' and having 'tasted the good word of God' (Heb. 6:4-5). Yet, there are those who turn their back on such things, and in doing so 'count the blood of the covenant by which he was sanctified a common thing, and insult the Spirit of grace' (Heb. 10:29, see also 2 Pet. 2:1). The Spirit that has been striving with them in common grace through the gospel offers of Christ (just as He did with Israel in the Old Testament e.g. Neh. 9:27-30, Isa. 63:10, Acts 7:51), has been resisted and refused. Because such great graces and privileges have been rejected there is 'worse punishment' (Heb. 10:29). But this judgment does not invalidate the love and kindness God showed in the gospel offer. Rather it shows the reality of that love. For only genuine grace and love can lead to greater responsibility. As John Murray comments on these verses, 'here we find non-saving grace at its very apex. We cannot conceive of anything, that falls short of salvation, more exalted in its character. And we must not make void the reality of the blessing enjoyed and of the grace bestowed out of consideration for the awful doom resultant upon … apostacy.'[14]

Conclusion

God shows grace and love to all in the world in many ways. He is gracious to all, and loves all in giving material gifts and restraining evil in the world. He expresses an even deeper grace and love to all who receive the gospel offer. This is the wonderful testimony of both the Old and New Testaments. To deny that God is favourably disposed to all in love and grace is to turn the scriptures on their head, and render its language meaningless. But, as genuine love and grace are shown to all, it should make everyone very careful not to reject them. For 'how shall we escape if we neglect so great a salvation?' (Heb. 2:3).

---

14. Murray, *Collected Writings*, 2:110.

8

OBJECTIONS CONSIDERED

What more do you have to say? Lay out your objections. These words 'all things are ready' will answer them all. The garment is ready to be put on, yea, Jesus Christ is your wedding garment; take and put Him on. He is the cure for all your diseases; apply Him for the cure of them all.
James Durham (1622-58)[1]

The doctrine of the free offer of the gospel outlined so far is liable to certain objections which need to be considered. These objections are both practical and theological. They range from individuals who struggle to hold together the sovereignty of God in salvation with the invitation to them to believe, to theologians who use the gospel offer to undermine God's sovereignty, to other theologians who use God's sovereignty to undermine the gospel offer!

Most of these critics of the gospel offer in one way or another take a scriptural truth and draw (supposedly) logical deductions from it to prevent scripture so clearly saying what it does in another area. For instance, if God has invited all to salvation then, according to this logic, He cannot have chosen only some

---

1. Durham, *Unsearchable Riches*, 76.

to eternal life, or from the other angle, if God has chosen only some to eternal life, then He cannot invite all sincerely to be saved. But this way of doing theology is wholly wrongheaded. We are never to abstract one truth from the context of scripture and deduce from that what the rest of the Bible must teach on a topic. Rather we take the holistic teaching of scripture, and accept it, in this case that God lovingly, graciously invites all to believe and be saved, while in sovereign love chooses some to everlasting life and enables them to believe. Whatever logical difficulties this causes, we submit ourselves to the scriptures and in faith seek an understanding of how both can be true, recognising 'it is not surprising that our eyes should be blinded by intense light, so that we cannot certainly judge how God wishes all to be saved, and yet has devoted all the reprobate to eternal destruction, and wishes them to perish.'[2] In that spirit we now turn to some common reasons (some of which have been considered incidentally in previous chapters) why people object to the teaching of a sincere invitation to salvation.

If I Am Dead in Sin Why Invite Me to Believe?

It is undeniably true that every sinner in the world is 'dead in trespasses and sins' (Eph. 2:1). The dead cannot bring life to themselves, and nor can dead sinners believe. Again, to turn from unbelief to belief is like to being 'born again' (John 3:3), and just as being born the first time is not within our own gift, neither is being 'born again'. As we are in ourselves, we are sinful from the time our mothers conceived us (Ps. 51:5). We are by nature subject to the 'carnal mind' which '*is* enmity against God; for it is not subject to the law of God, nor indeed can be' (Rom. 8:7). In the light of these scriptures, it is surely

---

2.   Calvin, *Calvin's Commentaries*, 12:247.

incontrovertible that we cannot believe through our own strength.

From this, some reason that since we cannot save ourselves, we are to do nothing. There is no point in giving the gospel offer, so the logic goes, because you don't go to a cemetery and invite the dead to live. From the point of view of the hearer of the gospel, we might argue that there is no point trying to receive the gospel offer, because, if God wants to save me He will, and if He doesn't there is nothing I can do about it because I am a dead sinner.

There are several things that can be said in relation to this. The first is that it is wrong to isolate this aspect of God's sovereignty from any other. It is not just that we cannot save ourselves apart from God's work, we cannot do anything apart from God. Think of God's declaration concerning sparrows: 'Not one of them falls to the ground apart from your Father's will' (Matt. 10:29). The same is surely true of all creatures. Do those who are gardeners and discover slugs attacking a hosta or a lettuce ask themselves whether the disposing, or deterring of these creatures is the will of God? No! Gardeners recognise that the good of their plants comes first. Sinners should recognise that the good of their souls should come before such religious scruples.

It is in God that 'we live and move and have our being' (Acts 17:28). We cannot live a day apart from God's sovereign will, and yet we eat, we drink, we exercise, all so that we continue to live. Indeed, we cannot do anything apart from God's sovereign work, as it is only 'If the Lord wills, we shall live and do this or that' (James 4:15). Yet we never use that as an excuse to refuse to do anything we want or believe we need to do. No one (at least no one I have met) reasons I can only go to the supermarket if it is God's will, so I'll sit here because if God wanted me to go, He will get me there and if He doesn't, well, I won't be able to get to the supermarket anyway. The foolishness of this is self-evident. Yet it is not unusual to hear people say if God wants to save me, He will save me, but if He doesn't then nothing will change that, so there is no point trying to believe. God's sovereignty involves using means to accomplish His will in every aspect of our lives, the gospel offer not excepted.

The second thing to reflect on is that the inability to believe is rooted not in any fundamental impossibility of believing (otherwise absolutely no one would believe), but is rather a determined wilful purpose not to believe. What prevents a response of faith? An unregenerate will. The truth is 'you are not willing to come to Me that you may have life' (John 5:40). God is willing to save, He earnestly offers salvation in the gospel, and places no hindrances in the way of any accepting it, for it is without money and without price. The blame for refusal to accept the gospel cannot be laid on God. Quite the reverse, God does so much to secure the gospel's acceptance that He has every right to ask, 'What more could have been done?' (Isa. 5:4). As Thomas Manton said, 'God is not the cause of man's destruction ... it is man's own fault if they be not converted and saved.'[3] No temptation, including the temptation to reject the gospel comes from God (James 1:13). Rather the rejection of the gospel is a positive, wholehearted, active rejection. It is not a passive sleep of death, but a living, aggressive, refusal to believe. This unwillingness to believe is evidenced in refusing to listen to the gospel, being apathetic to Christian testimony, wilfully rejecting Christ, and resisting common grace in the striving of the Spirit. No one can claim they were not responsible for their active rejection of Christ and His gospel.

The third point to make is that the gospel offer serves a purpose even for those who will not believe. It renders their

3.   Manton, *Works*, 21:471.

unbelief inexcusable, and removes the cloak that covers their sin. What excuse can those have, who do not believe the gospel, when it shall be found that they deliberately choose to reject it? It will be of no use to say, 'I could not believe,' since in response Jesus will simply say, 'How often I wanted to gather your children together, as a hen *gathers* her brood under *her* wings, but you were not willing' (Matt. 23:37). The gospel offer, to those dead in sins, reveals their sinful unwillingness to believe. Once that unwillingness and inability is revealed, far from leading to passivity, it should drive lost sinners to cry to God for the salvation they cannot bring to themselves, knowing that 'it is God who works in you both to will and to do for *His* good pleasure' (Phil. 2:13).

If God Has Chosen to Save Some Why Invite All to Believe?

A related objection comes from the doctrine of God's sovereign election. Again, it is a glorious truth that God is sovereign in salvation. It is true of everyone who is and will be saved that God 'saved us and called *us* with a holy calling, not according to our works, but according to His own purpose and grace which was given to us in Christ Jesus before time began' (2 Tim. 1:9). But if God has chosen to save some why are all offered salvation in the gospel? If 'few are chosen' why are 'many called' (Matt. 22:14)? This question has led some to the conclusion that they cannot believe until they know they are among the 'chosen few'. They argue that only those who are chosen will be saved, and so the gospel invitation should only be accepted once they know they have been predestined to salvation.

So, how do we respond to the objection 'I will not believe until I know I am elect'? Well, first by saying that no one ever knew they were elect until they believed. We read in Acts that 'as many as had been appointed to eternal life believed' (Acts 13:48). How do we know they were 'appointed to life'? Only because they believed. There is no list of the elect on earth. There is no way of knowing who will be saved, but by believing. If this is the barrier people place before believing, no one will ever be saved. And to show the foolishness of this reasoning, no one would then have been elected, because the elect are the believing and saved people of God! Any quest to place the knowledge of election prior to belief is simply to 'conceive of the decree of God, as of a deep policy and a stratagem and snare laid for us'.[4]

We can then move on to point people away from the secret will of God to His revealed will where He 'commands all people everywhere to repent' (Acts. 17:30). In the gospel invitation the hearer has nothing to do with the secret will (who is or is not predestined to believe) but has everything to do with the universal gospel invitation: 'Look to Me, and be saved, All you ends of the earth! For I *am* God, and *there is* no other' (Isa. 45:22). This is exactly the teaching of Deuteronomy 29:29: 'The secret *things belong* to the Lord our God, but those *things which are* revealed *belong* to us and to our children forever, that *we* may do all the words of this law.' We give our attention to what God has revealed He wants us to do, not what He may or may not have decreed regarding us. So, we are not to consider questions about election which can never be answered, but to listen to God's own assurances in scripture that He wants all to come to Him: 'I have no pleasure in the death of one who dies, says the Lord God. Therefore turn and live' (Ezek. 18:32). So, we aren't to use God's sovereign election as an excuse to reject the gospel. We are not to refuse obedience to a clear command, upon a secret decree, which we can never know except as we

---

4.   Samuel Rutherford, *Christ Dying and Drawing Sinners to Himself* (Repr., Edinburgh: T. Lumisden and J. Robertson, 1727), 522.

believe or refuse to believe. James Durham helpfully preached on this point:

> Objection… I do not know if I am one of God's elect… What is this? You do not well know what you say. Have you anything to do with that secret by a leap at the first hand. Are you not called to marry Christ? Is not this His revealed will to you? I protest in His name, this is the thing that you are called to; and will you make an exception where He has made none? Or will you shift obedience to a clear command, upon a supposed decree which you can not know but by the effects? Will you reason so in the matter of your eating and drinking? … will you this day refuse your dinner … Because you do not know if God has appointed you to live so and so long?[5]

We can also draw attention to the truth that election or non-election is not the ground for anyone's condemnation or judgment, but rather unbelief. No one can at the last say to God, I was not saved because I wasn't elect, it was your fault, not mine. In response God will simply say, 'Have you not brought this on yourself, In that you have forsaken the Lord your God When He led you in the way?' (Jer. 2:17). The gospel is like a bridge over a river. Its purpose is to take people safely across the river. It is not the fault of the bridge if people refuse to make use of it and thereby drown themselves. Election is no barrier to using the bridge, which is there for all who want to use it.

Finally, that God has chosen some to be saved is no impediment to God's right to call all to Him to be saved. He has a right to demand obedience from all, even if He will not give sovereign help to ensure obedience is given. Indeed, election spurs on the gospel invitation. Despite the hardness of hearts of humanity, God will use the preaching of the gospel message to save sinners, and that is a great encouragement to go

---

5. Durham, *Unsearchable Riches*, 76-77.

on inviting, to go on offering the gospel. God will use it to save. His election of some to life guarantees it!

If Jesus Only Died for His Sheep How Can All Be Invited to Believe?

Another related objection to the gospel offer flows from what is known as the doctrine of particular redemption. This doctrine teaches that Christ did not die with the intention that His atoning work would save all, but rather that He died to save His Church (Eph. 5:25) and His sheep (John 10:11). This, again, is the clear teaching of scripture. But it raises the question, if Jesus did not die for all, how can all be called on to believe? Indeed, how can anyone know that Jesus died for them if particular redemption is true?

To respond here we need to consider precisely what the gospel message is, and what it is we are called to believe in. When we do that, we will find that the extent of the atonement is not the central gospel message. We know that not all will be saved. If Christ died for all, as some claim, it is obvious that His death does not achieve the salvation of all. The central gospel message is that Christ died for sinners, even the very chief (1 Tim. 1:15); that there is no class or type of sin in the world beyond the power of Christ to save (John 1:29); that the blood of Christ cleanses from all sin (1 John 1:7); and that salvation is found only in Jesus for 'there is no other name under heaven given among men by which we must be saved' (Acts 4:12). We are invited to believe in the nature and efficacy of the atonement of Jesus, not the numerical extent of who, in God's purpose, it applies to. As W. G. T. Shedd has said:

> when God calls upon men universally to believe, he does not call upon them to believe that they are elected or that Christ died for them in particular. He calls them to believe that Christ

died for sin, for sinners, for the world; that there is no other name under heaven given among men whereby they must be saved; that the blood of Christ cleanses from all sin; that there is no condemnation to them that are in Christ Jesus... Men are commanded to believe in the sufficiency of the atonement, not in its predestined application to them as individuals.[6]

There is no insufficiency in Jesus' death. Every sinner who comes to Jesus will find His atonement sufficient to save them, for 'He is also able to save to the uttermost those who come to God through Him' (Heb. 7:25). Therefore, that Jesus died with the intent of redeeming His sheep is no barrier to all accepting the offer of Jesus in the gospel. He is the all sufficient and suitable Saviour of sinners, freely offered by God to us. That is what we are called to embrace by faith. Indeed, as John Murray has argued,

> The doctrine of election and the doctrine of limited atonement place no fence around the free offer. The free offer comes from the heart of God's sovereign will unto salvation, and it is definite atonement that grounds the kind of overture proclaimed in the gospel.[7]

If God Is Sovereign, and Not All Are Saved, Then Is God Not Insincere in His Invitation?

This question brings together the challenge of God's sovereign choice over who to save and His pleading with all unbelievers to embrace His offered salvation. It seems on the face of it inconsistent and possibly hypocritical to invite sinners to believe, and to beg them to do so, knowing they never will. This

---

6. Shedd, *Dogmatic Theology*, 752.
7. Murray, *Collected Writings*, 2:257.

is a real difficulty, perhaps the greatest difficulty in connection with the universal gospel invitation.

Indeed, to give a complete answer to this kind of objection is not possible. There comes a point where we simply have to stand silent before the question 'Can you search out the deep things of God? Can you find out the limits of the Almighty?' (Job 11:7) and realise that 'My thoughts *are* not your thoughts, Nor *are* your ways My ways... For *as* the heavens are higher than the earth, So are My ways higher than your ways, And My thoughts than your thoughts' (Isa. 55:8-9). But there is still much that we can say.

To begin with, we can realise that this question does not ultimately pose a unique difficulty. It is rather a particular application of the greater question of the existence of evil. The challenge of the existence of evil is often stated as follows: if God is good and all powerful, then how can we explain the existence of evil? Either God is powerful enough to prevent evil and chooses not to, in which case He is not good. Or He is good enough to prevent evil but lacks the power to do so, in which case He is not powerful, and so hardly worthy of being designated as God.

The similarity of this kind of reasoning to the question of the sincerity of the gospel offer in relation to God's sovereignty can be seen if we express the objection like this: if God is good and is also all-powerful, how can He express compassion for the lost in the gospel offer yet fail to ensure that multitudes will not be lost? Phrased like this, challenges to God's sincerity in His gospel offers become a specific application of the greater question of the existence of evil.

To answer the specific question on the sincerity of the gospel offer, we can see first that just as the Bible never views God's goodness or sovereignty as incompatible with a fallen sinful word, neither does it allow us to see God's sovereignty as incompatible with a genuine gospel invitation. We have this clearly revealed to us in Isaiah 5. We have considered this passage several times before. God pictures His people as a vineyard. He has done everything that this vineyard could possibly need to be productive. It has been planted in a fruitful place. The ground had been cleared and tended well. The vine stock used to plant the vineyard is the very best. (Isa. 5:1-2). And yet no good fruit came from the vineyard: 'it brought forth wild grapes' (Isa. 5:2). The parallel with Israel is so very clear. They had 'the adoption, the glory, the covenants, the giving of the law, the worship, and the promises' (Rom. 9:4, ESV) and yet despite all this they rejected their God and Saviour. God has given Israel everything humanly possible to save them, and they continually rejected Him, so that God could truly and legitimately say, 'What more could have been done to My vineyard That I have not done in it?' (Isa. 5:4).

Now the obvious implication of this question for Israel is that they could not throw back the repose, 'You haven't done all. You could have converted us by your almighty power, so no you haven't done all for us.' Clearly when Israel have rejected every good thing God has done for them, actively and wilfully, they cannot accuse God of not doing enough, or of not being sincere in His desire for fruit. When every move of God's common grace and love has been despised, there is no recourse to claiming God should have done more, or that He didn't really want them to produce fruit. Thomas Manton comments:

> the blame cannot lie in God… [God] offered you grace in him [Christ], pardon of all your sins… moved you by powerful arguments… the joys of heaven, the torments of hell; called upon you often by the ministry, knocked at your hearts as well

as your ears by his Spirit... tried you by mercies if they could melt you... What more shall God do?[8]

Therefore, Isaiah 5 tells us that the Bible takes human accountability and responsibility very seriously. God's sovereignty does not, with apologies to Shakespeare, turn life into 'a tale told by an idiot, full of sound and fury, signifying nothing.'[9] Blessings in this life matter; they are sincerely given by God for good. What we do with them matters. When we reject what God has given us that is not because God is insincere in offering us the gospel, or inviting us to accept it, or pleading with us to embrace salvation. The insincerity is not in God; His offer and desire are genuine. The fault in rejecting it is ours, and ours alone. God, in a very important sense, could do no more for us. If we question the sincerity of this, our quarrel is with God.

This leads to an important observation. In the words of W. G. T. Shedd, 'sincerity depends upon the intrinsic nature of the thing desired, not upon the results of the endeavours to attain it.'[10] There is no insincerity in God because He is compassionate, merciful and loving in pleading for sinners to embrace the gospel, even although He has not decreed that it must take place. The embrace of the gospel in faith and repentance, would be pleasing to God. It is true, not hypocritical, to say that God will rejoice in the conversion of any and every sinner. When God in compassion cries out, 'Turn, turn from your evil ways! For why should you die, O house of Israel? (Ezek. 33:11), that is absolutely sincere, because God always delights in obedience rather than disobedience.

---

8. Manton, *Works*, 21:471-2.
9. William Shakespeare, *Macbeth: A Tragedy in Five Acts* (New York: Seer's Printing Establishment, 1880), 101.
10. Shedd, *Dogmatic Theology*, 346.

The case that God is insincere in the gospel invitation would be a strong one if God was actively hindering sinners from accepting the invitation. That would be hypocrisy. But that is not the case. God does not work in any to cause them to reject the gospel. He may leave individuals increasingly to their own sin and hardness of heart (as Pharaoh), but God does not actively cause any to sin in failing to believe in Jesus (John 16:9). Instead God's Spirit strives with sinners that they might believe (Gen. 6:3, Heb. 6:4), and every inducement to believe is given as God shows common love and grace. It cannot be shown that God is insincere, simply because He does not proceed to give saving grace.

We can go further and say that the assumption underlying this objection is that God cannot genuinely show any compassion and sincerity in the gospel to an individual unless He shows special saving grace. But this assumption simply does not hold true. To be sincere in inviting someone does not mean that we have to ensure someone's acceptance. In calling His saved people to be holy as He is holy (1 Pet. 1:16) is God insincere? Does God not have it in His power to keep His people from falling into sin? Does God not desire His people conform exactly to the image of His Son? Yes, God wants this, and has the power to do it, but He doesn't. Again, He is not insincere in this, it is just that in His wisdom He sees reasons not to immediately make His people perfectly holy, even though He commands and wants this.

The mystery of God's will is seen in the case of Judas. Although Jesus said, 'And truly the Son of Man goes as it has been determined, but woe to that man by whom He is betrayed!' (Luke 22:22), yet Judas was present when Jesus taught the disciples about Himself and when He gave the free gospel invitations already considered. We can speculate on the reasons for Judas' betrayal, but neither they nor the truth that

Satan entered Judas' heart (John 13:2) affect the twin truths that Judas played his part according to the divine plan and that he was responsible for his actions in betraying rather than loving Jesus. Jesus had washed his feet in love and Jesus had warned him, yet Judas went to his doom. Faced with this mystery, we can only acknowledge the inscrutable nature of God's will and the folly of human rejection of divine love. We can take the general principle that just because God has the power to do something, His wisdom regulates the exercise of that power, without making Him insincere.

To reflect on this further, let us consider an individual God has given the gospel invitation to. He has pleaded with that individual to accept the invitation (2 Cor. 5:20). His Spirit has striven with the individual to make the person accept (Gen. 6:3). But this is rejected. The gospel is spurned. Now, up to this point has God not shown this sinner love, grace and mercy? Has He not done everything He could for this vineyard to produce fruit? Has God done one thing to tempt this individual to sin (James 1:13)? Has He done one thing that points to a lack of sincerity in the gospel invitation? Is God obliged to go on and show further love and grace in order for what He has done up to this point to be loving and merciful? Surely not. We cannot say that if God shows any mercy and love to a sinner, He is obliged to show all mercy and love. We can love all our neighbours, without loving them in the way we love our spouses and children. It is no less so with God. Someone who has rejected the loving gospel invitation cannot go on to call God insincere because He does not continue to show more grace and love in conversion.

To conclude, we need to take God seriously when it is said: 'God *is* not a man, that He should lie, Nor a son of man, that He should repent. Has He said, and will He not do? Or has He spoken, and will He not make it good?' (Num. 23:19).

There is no falsehood in God. Therefore, when God declares on oath, *'As I live, says the Lord God, I have no pleasure in the death of the wicked, but that the wicked turn from his way and live. Turn, turn from your evil ways! For why should you die, O house of Israel?'* (Ezek. 33:11) we are simply to take Him at His word. It might be hard for us to reconcile this with God's sovereignty, but that is no basis for us to reject the clear teachings of scripture. When the gospel offer is proclaimed, we are simply to recognise that it does sincerely disclose God's benevolence. As W. G. T. Shedd has rightly said:

> The fact that God does not in the case of the non-elect bestow special grace to overcome the resisting self-will that renders the gifts of providence and common grace ineffectual does not prove that he in insincere in his desire that man would believe… any more than the fact that a benevolent man declines to double the amount of his gift, after the gift already offered has been spurned, proves he did not sincerely desire that the person would take the sum first offered.[11]

Isn't God's Desire for the Gospel to Be Accepted By All Ineffectual, Leaving His Love and Grace Hopelessly Frustrated?

We have seen that God delights in the salvation of sinners, and shows love and grace to those He doesn't ultimately save. We have also seen God's sovereignty, the truth that *'our God is* in heaven; He does whatever pleases Him'* (Ps. 115:3). The question here sets these two truths in opposition and alleges that if God really shows grace and love to sinners then He would save them and if He didn't that would simply show God

---

11. Shedd, *Dogmatic Theology*, 349.

is not powerful enough to do what He wants, leaving His love and grace frustrated.

In response, the first point to note is the complexity this kind of dichotomy fails to recognise. It is absolutely right that God does nothing ineffectual. When God purposes to do a thing, He does it, 'for who has resisted His will?' (Rom. 9:19). But, again, the situation is far more involved than it first appears. We cannot use verses like Psalm 115:3 to ride roughshod over the plain teaching of the rest of scripture. To return to earlier trains of thought, does God want me to love my neighbour as myself? Would that please Him? Yes, absolutely. Does my sin in failing to do so displease Him? Again, obviously yes. But somehow mysteriously that does not contradict Psalm 115, nor does Psalm 115 contradict the truth that God is displeased with sin. This question of the 'frustration' of the grace of God in the gospel offer is no different to the question of the frustration of God's desire in connection with any aspect of His revealed will.

But secondly, and more importantly, while it is possible to 'frustrate' the gospel offer in one sense (2 Cor. 6:1) the gospel offer is not ineffectual. It accomplishes everything God intends it to. It presses home His sovereignty over all sinners. God has a right to command all everywhere to repent and believe the gospel, and the gospel offer demonstrates this. Further, under the blessing of His Spirit, it saves a multitude which no one can number from all nations (Rev. 7:9). Through it, God saves His people. Again, it reveals His genuine love, compassion, and mercy to all. God in kindness sends the message of the good news as a blessing, and accompanies it with many other common graces as we have seen. God's goodness, His love and grace, are revealed in the gospel offer, however it is received. Let God's character be true and every man a liar (Rom. 3:4). Finally, God's justice is vindicated. God's gospel offer to all stops every mouth, and every accusation that might be made against Him in condemning sinners. None of these ends are frustrated by the gospel being rejected.

If we persist and say that God's desire that sinners repent, believe and be saved is incompatible with Him allowing sinners to reject His love, well, again, this is just the age-old problem we have touched on of how a good, holy and powerful God can allow sin. To fully solve that question, we wait for eternity!

God Hates the Wicked. How Can He Then Be Said to Love Them in the Gospel Invitation?

This objection to the gospel invitation is based on an assumption that God cannot be said to love and hate an individual at the same time. Given this assumption, if God 'hates' an individual so as not to save them (Rom. 9:13) He cannot be favourably disposed or gracious or loving to them in any way. However, this objection does not fit the teaching of scripture.

If we reverse the argument, we can see its problems. While God loves His people, He certainly expresses wrath towards them and is angry with them. Before they are saved God's people are eternally loved (Eph. 1:4-5), and yet they are 'by nature children of wrath, just as the others' (Eph. 2:3). Until that time when they are made 'alive together with Christ' (Eph. 2:5) God's own people are under the wrath of God. This is the same teaching as John 3 where until someone believes they are in a state of 'condemnation' (John 3:18) and under the 'wrath of God' (John 3:36). Similarly, Moses 'the man of God' (Deut. 33:1) could say, 'We have been consumed by Your anger, And by Your wrath we are terrified' (Ps. 90:7). Clearly those whom God loves savingly are not just the objects of love (though they are always loved!). So, why should it be that those who never believe are always and only the recipients of God's wrath? Just as God hates the elect whom He loves while they are 'workers of iniquity' (Ps. 5:5), so He loves the wicked who remain His enemies (Matt. 5:44-45).

Various illustrations can help us see how this can be. Take the example of a judge who has before him a friend he has loved all his life, now guilty of a great crime. From the perspective of the law the friend is now under condemnation and judicial wrath. But even as the judge executes the sentence with the full vigour of the law, the love of years of friendship may remain. Or take the example of two soldiers who fought side by side, who bled together, who saw friends die together. Years later, one of them is presiding over a court martial where his friend is under trial for desertion. Though as presiding officer he has to pass the full weight of the judicial sentence, this does not mean that pronouncing a severe sentence is incompatible with the bonds of love formed over past years.

So, there is no reason to object to God loving those whom in one sense He hates. We are free to accept the manifold testimony of scripture, that God has a love to those He decreed not to save, and this is expressed in the gospel offer.

Rejecting the Gospel Offer Leads to Greater Condemnation. How Then Can it Be Love and Grace?

It is undeniable that the rejection of the gospel will lead to greater condemnation: 'For everyone to whom much is given, from him much will be required; and to whom much has been committed, of him they will ask the more' (Luke 12:48). The warning is a solemn one: 'Whoever will not receive you nor hear your words... Assuredly, I say to you, it will be more tolerable for the land of Sodom and Gomorrah in the day of judgment than for that city!' (Matt. 10:14-15). Rejecting the gospel is a great and grievous sin, for it is to count the blood of Christ an unholy thing, and carelessly spurn the tender appeals of the gospel to find mercy through the slain Lamb of God. It therefore carries with it a great weight of judgment.

But this doesn't in any way overturn the nature of the gospel invitation as a good, loving gift. The nature of the gospel offer itself remains a good and gracious gift, while it is the perverseness of the recipients that turns it into a cause for judgment. Indeed, in order for the gospel invitation to be the means of bringing greater judgment, it must in itself remain a good thing. It is only because the gospel is an expression of grace and love that its rejection leads to greater condemnation. It is only the reality of the grace demonstrated that leads to the result of greater accountability: 'it is just because they are good gifts and manifestations of the kindness and mercy of God that the abuse of them brings greater condemnation and demonstrated the greater inexcusability of impenitence.'[12]

Again, we cannot use God's sovereign superintendence over all of this to gut history and the Bible of meaning. We cannot say that because God knows and has ordained that some will perish everlastingly, and knows that the gospel offer will increase their condemnation, it is not still a kind and good thing to offer salvation in Christ to all. We know we cannot say this because the Bible doesn't. Nowhere in scripture do matters of God's secret will and decree override the reality of God's dealings in time. We cannot allow election or non-election to so warp our understanding that the simple and straightforward teaching of scripture is dismissed. John Murray helpfully comments,

> The decree of reprobation is of course undeniable. But denial of the reality of temporal goodness and kindness ... as expressions of the mind and will of God, is to put the

12. Murray, *Collected Writings*, 2:106.

decree of reprobation so much out of focus that it eclipses the straightforward testimony of scripture to other truths.[13]

The scriptures are reliable when they say that 'the riches of His goodness, forbearance, and longsuffering' are being shown even to those who are 'in accordance with your hardness and your impenitent heart ... treasuring up for yourself wrath in the day of wrath and revelation of the righteous judgment of God' (Rom. 2:4-5). It is not a lie when the psalmist sings, 'The Lord *is* good to all, And His tender mercies *are* over all His works' (Ps. 145:9). It is no falsehood to see the sun and rain, temporal mercies, as expressions of God's love (Matt. 5:44-45). No fallacious deductions from God's decree can make the scripture false. The gospel is a blessing because of what it is in itself. It is love that bestows it as a gift. And it remains so, however it is abused.

Conclusion

The objections to the sincere gospel invitation are many and varied. But the testimony of scripture is plain. God invites all to come to Him, pleads with all to come to Him, and sincerely displays His love and grace in doing so.

---

13. Murray, *Collected Writings*, 2:106.

CONCLUSION

*If we fail to appreciate what the free offer of the gospel is, and if
we fail to present this free offer with freedom and spontaneity,
with passion and urgency, then we are not only doing dishonour
to Christ and his glory but we are also choking those who are
the candidates of saving faith. It is only in reference to the full
and free overture of Christ in the gospel that a true conception of
faith in Christ can be entertained.*
John Murray (1898-1975)[1]

The gospel is a glorious thing: Jesus Christ proclaimed as the
only Saviour of sinners with invitations and pleadings to come
to Him, giving all a right to accept the Saviour so freely offered
in the gospel. It is a gospel message so full of love and grace to
all, expressive of the desire of God that all come and be saved.
What a wonderful message for a lost world! However, it is a
message that is perhaps not as evident in churches that delight
in the sovereignty of God as it should be. Therefore, drawing
to a close, there are some points that should be considered in
applying the gospel offer today.

---

1. John Murray, *Collected Writings of John Murray* (4 vols.; Edinburgh:
Banner of Truth, 1976-1982), 1:147.

Exhortations to Come to Christ

A key feature of the best of preaching in the past was repeated and frequent appeals to sinners to come to Christ for salvation. Here is one example from a great seventeenth-century preacher:

> Our blessed Lord Jesus is wooing you ... our Lord Jesus is not far to seek, He is here waiting on to close the bargain with you: This is our errand to proclaim these glad tidings to you ... Is not the Father ready? He hath given his consent; is not the Bridegroom ready, when He hath done so much and is waiting on your consent? the Feast is ready, and the Garments are ready ... the contract is ready ... He is ready to accept of you, if ye will accept of him; our blessed Lord Jesus says that He is content to marry you ... there is in effect nothing wanting but your consent, and let that not be wanting, I beseech you.[2]

Like this example, all gospel preaching and witnessing should highlight a willing Saviour, a willing Father, and a sincere and open offer of salvation to all. There should be a genuine pleading with hearers that the gospel invitation be accepted. All should be pleaded with not to receive the grace of the gospel offer in vain. The role of preachers (and individual Christians) is never to simply or dispassionately outline facts (if you believe you will be saved, if you don't you will not) but to warmly and with tears in our eyes persuade sinners to come to Christ. If it pleases God to save sinners primarily through the foolishness of preaching (1 Cor. 1:21, KJV), then it is not enough to say at the close of a sermon something like, 'if you are interested in a personal relationship with Jesus please speak to me, or one of the team'. The very preaching itself should be full of the same pleadings as that of the apostle Paul, 'as though God were pleading through us: we implore you on Christ's behalf, be reconciled to God' (2 Cor. 5:20). We need more of the spirit of Thomas Boston

---

2.   Durham, *Unsearchable Riches,* 56.

who wrote, 'It is the great work of ministers, to compel sinners, in a gospel-way, to come in to Christ.'[3]

Hell

Preaching (and explaining) the gospel invitation should be accompanied with clarity on the reality of hell. There should be frequent warnings accompanying the gospel invitation that if Christ, as He is offered in the gospel, is rejected there is no escape from hell. Every person outside Christ is in danger of hell. We, and they, should be left in no doubt about this. This should lead us to earnestly seek to bring men and women to faith: 'Knowing, therefore, the terror of the Lord, we persuade men' (2 Cor. 5:11). There should be no hiding of the awful consequences of rejecting Christ, 'To be slain, and die before Christ, who died to save sinners, is a thousand deaths in one; it is a hell upon a hell ... no flame of wrath will pierce into a damned soul, like that which is blown up by the breath of a slighted mediator.'[4]

There is little doubt that our passion for the gospel invitation, the effort and pathos with which we proclaim the good news, and our belief in and emphasis on the realities of eternal life and death are related. Our lack of emphasis on one or the other will not reflect well on our faithfulness to our Lord.

Conviction of Sin

Related to an emphasis on the reality of hell, there should be an emphasis that the rejection of the free offer of the gospel is a great and significant sin. To reject the gospel is to sin against grace, against love, against Jesus as the divine-human Saviour

---

3. Boston, *Works*, 6:280.
4. Boston, *Works*, 6:290.

of sinners and ultimately against God. Consequently, this sinning in rejecting the gospel offer is greater than any other sin committed against the law, and will be punished more severely than any other sin. No one should be left in any doubt of this. No other sins, no matter however prevalent in society, compare with this one:

> Woe to you, Chorazin! Woe to you, Bethsaida! For if the mighty works which were done in you had been done in Tyre and Sidon, they would have repented long ago in sackcloth and ashes. But I say to you, it will be more tolerable for Tyre and Sidon in the day of judgment than for you. And you, Capernaum, who are exalted to heaven, will be brought down to Hades; for if the mighty works which were done in you had been done in Sodom, it would have remained until this day. But I say to you that it shall be more tolerable for the land of Sodom in the day of judgment than for you. (Matt. 11:21-24)

Doubting Discouraged

There is a natural tendency where God's sovereignty is believed to use that as an excuse to refuse to believe. After all if 'few are chosen' (Matt. 22:14) then I might not well be among them. However, the gospel offer with its freedom should be used to discourage this kind of unbiblical doubting. No one is entitled to despairing or doubtful thoughts as long as they have the free offer of the gospel. The gospel offer should be used to testify to all that it is pleasing to God to save sinners, even the chief, and so none should despair over the possibility of their own salvation. Election and particular redemption can and must be preached and explained, but should never be explained in a way that detracts from the revealed will of God that all should come to Him for salvation. Gospel preaching should carry the note,

'He is able to save you... He is willing to save you... The only thing wanting [lacking] is your willingness to be saved.'[5]

Urgency

The gospel invitation should be presented with urgency. There should be an insistence on an immediate response to the gospel offer. No delay should be allowable: the only acceptable response should be an instantaneous acceptance of Christ. It is impossible to hear the gospel without either rejecting it and hardening ourselves against it, or accepting it. Yes, there must be patience and wisdom. There must be building of relationships. But when the gospel offer is preached the need to accept it now should be pressed home. There should be no doubt that we are dealing with matters of life and death. Delay is not acceptable, and can be fatal. Thomas Boston again provides a model for us:

> We dare not allow you a day, nay nor an hour, to think on it, whether ye will come or not; lest the next day, or the next hour, ye be cast into hell, or a hell be cast into you, for refusing the offer made to you at this moment... Wherefore delay no longer; but this moment open the everlasting doors that the King of glory may come in.[6]

An Appeal to Faith

Even though sinners lack the ability to believe, they must be called to faith. We all remain responsible for our sin, and our inability to come to Christ in faith is, as we have seen, more properly described as an unwillingness. Further, although faith is the gift of God, it remains our act and ours alone. God never

---

5. Boston, *Works*, 6:290.
6. Boston, *Works*, 6:289.

believes for us. Therefore, in preaching, hearers must be called to faith in the Christ who is offered in the gospel.

Think of the incident of Jesus and the man with the withered hand to understand this call to saving faith (Matt. 12:9-14). Christ asked the man to stretch out his hand, even though he could not (Matt. 12:13). Yet, in the 'impossible' act of trying to stretch out his hand in obedience to the command, it was healed. Just like this, even though we cannot believe, by grace, in the act of responding to the call to believe we will be enabled to believe. All need to be called to this.

Summary

The gospel invitation is a great treasure. But it is not a treasure to be hidden. Rather it is for all the world. It reveals the heart of God for lost and perishing sinners. It exalts Jesus Christ as the only Saviour of sinners, proclaims the wonder of His person and the perfection of His once for all satisfaction for sin. It cries out 'Behold! The Lamb of God who takes away the sin of the world!' (John 1:29). No one else can carry this message but ourselves. This is our privilege and calling:

> You are the light of the world. A city that is set on a hill cannot be hidden. Nor do they light a lamp and put it under a basket, but on a lampstand, and it gives light to all who are in the house. Let your light so shine before men, that they may see your good works and glorify your Father in heaven (Matt. 5:14-16).

May we all be enabled to be that light we are called to be, and in preaching or in witnessing (as our Christian calling dictates) to say to the world, 'Come, for all things are now ready' (Luke 14:17).

FURTHER READING

Below I present a small sample of historic works that may be helpfully consulted on the free offer of the gospel, common grace, and related matters to demonstrate the truths expressed in this book. Take up and read!

John Murray (1898–1975), an exceptional exponent of the free offer of the gospel.

Collected Writings of John Murray (4 vols.; Edinburgh: Banner of Truth, 1976-1982), in particular:
- 'The Atonement and the Free Offer of the Gospel', 1:59-85
- 'Some Necessary Emphases in Preaching', 1:143-151
- 'Common Grace', 2:93-119
- 'Faith', 2:255-7
- 'The Free Offer of the Gospel', 4:113-132 (also available as a stand-alone booklet by the same publisher)

Louis Berkhof (1873–1957), a classic systematiser of the Reformed faith, who had to defend the free offer of the gospel in ecclesiastical conflict.

Systematic Theology (Grand Rapids: Eerdmans, 1996), in particular:

- 'Common Grace', 432-46
- 'External Calling', 459-64

W. G. T. Shedd (1820–1894), a wonderful historical and systematic theologian, who defended the Westminster Confession against attempts to revise it in the American Presbyterian Church.

Dogmatic Theology (3rd edition; Ed. Alan W. Gomes; Phillipsburg: P&R Publishing, 2003), in particular:

- 'Reprobation' 333-44
- 'Objections to Election and Reprobation Answered', 346-9
- 'Universal Offer of the Atonement', 750-4

Calvinism Pure and Mixed (1893; Repr., Edinburgh: Banner of Truth, 1999), in particular:

- 'The Westminster Standards and the Universal Offer of Mercy', 23-28
- 'Common and Special Grace', 92-101

R. L. Dabney (1820–1898), one of the most profound theologians in the Reformed tradition. Some of his social views, stamped with the more extreme excesses of the racism of his day are abhorrent, but they do not appear in his theological reflections. Dabney goes as far as is possible while remaining 'orthodox' in his support of the gospel offer.

'God's Indiscriminate Proposals of Mercy, as Related to his Power, Wisdom, and Sincerity', in *Discussions Evangelical and*

Theological (2 vols.; 1891; Repr., Edinburgh: Banner of Truth, 1967), 282-313.

Systematic Theology (1871; Repr., Edinburgh: Banner of Truth, 1996), in particular:
• 'Effectual Calling', 553-9.

Robert Murray M'Cheyne (1813–1843), one of the great preachers of the gospel of the sovereign grace of God in Jesus Christ.

Memoir and Remains of Robert Murray M'Cheyne (Andrew A. Bonar, ed.; 1892; Repr., Edinburgh: Banner of Truth, 1966), in particular:
• 'The Gospel Call', 365-371
• 'Action Sermon', 467-73, especially 472 on Jesus tears over Jerusalem.

Additional Remains of the Rev. Robert Murray M'Cheyne (Edinburgh: John Johnstone, 1847), in particular:
• 'Jesus' compassion on the multitudes', 149-156
• 'If any man thirst', 295-302
• 'Ye will not come', 428-32

A Basket of Fragments (1848; Repr., Fearn: Christian Focus, 1975), in particular:
• 'Ministers Ambassadors of Christ', 9-12
• 'The Saviour's Tears over the Lost', 92-7

Charles Hodge (1797–1878), perhaps the most significant of the nineteenth-century Presbyterian theologians, teaching generations of ministers at Princeton Seminary. A defender of

Reformed theology as expressed in the Westminster Confession of Faith.

Systematic Theology (1872-3; 3 vols.; Repr., Peabody, MA: Hendrickson Publishers, 2003), in particular:

- 'External Call', 2:641-53
- 'Common Grace', 2:654-74

Princeton Sermons (1879; Repr., Edinburgh: Banner of Truth, 1979), in particular:

- 'The Tender Mercies of God', 14-16
- 'God so Loved the World', 16-18
- 'Who will have all men to be saved, and to come unto the knowledge of the truth', 18-19
- 'Come unto me, all ye that labour and are heavy laden, and I will give you rest', 129-31

Thomas Chalmers (1780–1847), the leading founder of the Free Church of Scotland. A profound theologian, preacher and leader of men.

Posthumous Works of the Rev. Thomas Chalmers Volume 6: Sermons by the Late Thomas Chalmers (William Hanna, ed.; New York: Harper and Brothers, 1849), in particular:

- 'The Embassy of Reconciliation', 338-55
- 'Fury not in God', 454-72

Posthumous Works of the Rev. Thomas Chalmers Volume 8: Institutes of Theology, Volume 2 (William Hanna, ed.; New York: Harper and Brothers, 1849), in particular:

- 'On the Preaching of Christ Crucified, as the great vehicle for the lessons of a Full and Free Gospel', 100-21
- 'On the Warrant which each man has to appropriate the Calls of the Gospel to himself, and what that is which marks his doing so', 262-70
- 'On the Universality of the Gospel', 418-28

Select Works of Thomas Chalmers Volume 4: Sermons, Volume 2 (William Hanna, ed.; Edinburgh: Edmonston and Douglas, 1872), in particular:
- 'On the Universality of the Gospel Offer', 450-62

Sermons and Discourses (2 vols.; New York: Robert Carter, 1844), in particular:
- 'On the Paternal Character of God', 1:7-12
- 'On the Spirit's Striving with Man', 1:35-42

Thomas Boston (1676–1732), one of Scotland's most profound theologians and defender of the free offer of the gospel.

The Complete Works of Thomas Boston (ed. Samuel M'Millan; 12 vols.; London: William Tegg and Co., 1854), in particular:
- 'A Caveat Against Receiving the Gospel in Vain', 2:443-54
- 'The Danger of Not Complying with the Gospel Call', 2:454-60
- 'Christ Demanding Admission into Sinners' Hearts', 3:93-117
- 'Present Room for Sinners in Christ's House', 3:260-71
- 'Farewell Sermon at Simprin', 4:458-65
- 'A Soliloquy on the Art of Man Fishing', 5:5-43
- 'Compel them to Come In', 6:279-93

- 'Christ the Saviour of the World', 6:294-305
- 'The Faith of the gospel offer', 8:587-91
- 'The Faith of our right to Christ', 8:591-7
- 'The Folly of Resisting, The Wisdom of Complying with the Gospel Call', 9:37-44
- 'Christ's Invitation to the Labouring and Heavy-Laden', 9:169-219
- 'God's Gracious Call and Precious Promise Considered', 9:482-90
- 'Christ, the Son of God, Gifted to Sinners', 10:188-202

Andrew Gray (1634–1656), an exceptional preacher in the days of full commitment to the Westminster Standards among the leadership of the Church of Scotland. Gray died at twenty-two but his sermons have been prized ever since his death and show Scottish preaching of the gospel invitation at its finest.

Loving Christ and Fleeing Temptation (ed. J.R. Beeke and K. Van Wyck; Grand Rapids: Reformation Heritage Books, 2007), in particular:

- 'Christ's Mournful Visit to Obstinate Sinners', 28-35
- 'The Necessity and Advantage of Looking unto Jesus', 574-86

Be Reconciled With God: Sermons of Andrew Gray (ed. J.R. Beeke; Grand Rapids: Reformation Heritage Books, 2019), in particular:

- 'Christ's Treaty of Peace with Sinners', 1-16
- 'Christ's Invitation to the Heavy Laden', 17-32

John Flavel (1630–1691), one of the most significant Puritan preachers and theologians.

The Works of John Flavel (6 vols.; 1820; Repr., Edinburgh: Banner of Truth, 1968), in particular:

- 'The Admirable Love of God in Giving His own Son for us', 1:62-71. While Flavel identifies the 'world' with the elect that does not prevent him speaking of love and mercy to those who reject Christ
- 'The Nature and Use of Gospel Ministry as an external Means of applying Christ: II Corinthians 5:20', 2:49-66
- 'England's Duty Under the Present Gospel Liberty: Eleven Sermons on Revelation 3:20', 4:17-267

James Durham (1622–1658), one of the greatest preachers and theologians of the mid-seventeenth-century Scottish church. For a full treatment of Durham, see Donald John MacLean, *James Durham (1622-1658): And the Gospel Offer in its Seventeenth Century Context* (Göttingen: Vandenhoeck & Ruprecht, 2015).

Collected Sermons of James Durham: 61 Sermons (Grand Rapids: Reformation Heritage Books, 2017), in particular:

- 'Matthew 22:2-4. *All things are ready; come to the marriage*', 464-85
- 'Isaiah 55:1-3, *I will make an everlasting covenant with you, even the sure mercies of David*', 518-32

Collected Sermons of James Durham: 72 Sermons on Isaiah 53 (Grand Rapids: Reformation Heritage Books, 2017), in particular:

- 'Sermons 1' through 'Sermon 10', 83-170 where topics such as 'Of the gospel call and the largeness of the offer,' 'All hearers have a warrant to believe,' 'Believing both command and required' and many others are discussed.

Commentary Upon the Book of the Revelation (Willow Street, PA: Old Paths, 2000), in particular:
- 'The Letter to the Church in Laodicea', 266-81

Thomas Manton (1620–1677), one of the most significant of the English Puritans, and author of the 'Epistle to the Reader' printed with the Westminster Standards.

The Complete Works of Thomas Manton (22 vols; 1870-5; Repr., Edinburgh: Banner of Truth, 2020), in particular:
- 'Sermon on Deuteronomy 30:15', 2:357-69
- 'Sermon on John 3:16', 2:340-57
- 'Now then, we are ambassadors for Christ, as though God did...' 13:290-305
- 'Sermons Upon Mark 10:17-27', 16:456-68
- 'Sermon Upon Acts 17:30-31', 16:397-408
- 'Several Sermons Upon Titus 2:11-14', 16:44, 54-68
- 'Sermons Upon Luke 19:10', 18:155-70
- 'Sermon Upon 2 Peter 3:9', 18:226-35
- 'Sermon Upon Matthew 22:14', 20:353-63
- 'Sermons Upon Ezekiel 18:23', 21:463-79

John Calvin (1509–1564), one of the greatest expositors and theologians in the Reformed tradition. His treatments of the gospel offer are exceptionally helpful and balanced. (For a full treatment of Calvin, see Donald John MacLean, 'John Calvin and the Gospel Offer,' in *Scottish Bulletin of Evangelical Theology* 34:1 (Autumn 2016).)

Calvin's Commentaries (22 vols.; Repr.; Grand Rapids: Baker, 1981), in particular comments on the scripture passages considered in this work, for example:
- Ezekiel 18:23
- Matthew 23:37
- John 3:16
- Romans 5:18
- 2 Peter 3:19

Institutes of the Christian Religion (Ed. John T. McNeill; Trans. F. L. Battles; 1559 ed.; 2 vols.; Louisville: Westminster John Knox Press, 1960), in particular:
- 'The Promise of Faith Fulfilled in Christ', Section 3.2.32, 1:579
- 'The manner of the call itself…' Section 3.24.2, 2:967
- 'General and Special Calling', Section 3.24.8, 2:974

COMPEL
THEM TO
COME IN

Calvinism and the
Free Offer of the Gospel

✝

DONALD
MACLEOD

Compel Them to Come In

Calvinism and the Free Offer of the Gospel

Donald Macleod

If we believe in God's sovereign predestination, how can we offer Christ to sinners indiscriminately? How could someone who knew that no one can come to Christ unless the Father draws them still plead with them to look to the Saviour? The Bible clearly entreats us to go after the lost, so Donald Macleod tackles the objections raised by those who argue that since there is no universal redemption there should be no universal gospel offer.

I always enjoy reading Donald MacLeod, as much for the clarity and precision of his arguments as for the elegance of his theology. Here he addresses an important topic – the free offer of the gospel – with his usual pungency and passion. It will clarify the issue for those who believe in the free offer but are confused by its connection to God's sovereignty; and it will hopefully persuade those who are tempted to truncate God's grace in a misguided attempt to exalt his election.

Carl R. Trueman
Professor of Biblical and Religious Studies, Grove City College,
Pennsylvania

ISBN 978-1-5271-0524-9

Christian Focus Publications

Our mission statement –

STAYING FAITHFUL
In dependence upon God we seek to impact the world through literature faithful to His infallible Word, the Bible. Our aim is to ensure that the Lord Jesus Christ is presented as the only hope to obtain forgiveness of sin, live a useful life and look forward to heaven with Him.

Our books are published in four imprints:

CHRISTIAN FOCUS

Popular works including biographies, commentaries, basic doctrine and Christian living.

CHRISTIAN HERITAGE

Books representing some of the best material from the rich heritage of the church.

MENTOR

Books written at a level suitable for Bible College and seminary students, pastors, and other serious readers. The imprint includes commentaries, doctrinal studies, examination of current issues and church history.

CF4•K

Children's books for quality Bible teaching and for all age groups: Sunday school curriculum, puzzle and activity books; personal and family devotional titles, biographies and inspirational stories – because you are never too young to know Jesus!

Christian Focus Publications Ltd,
Geanies House, Fearn, Ross-shire,
IV20 1TW, Scotland, United Kingdom.
www.christianfocus.com